THE COMPLETE
VEGETARIAN
KETO Diet
Cookbook for Everyday

Low-Carb, High-Fat Vegetarian Recipes for Beginners on the Ketogenic Diet

Christian Robinson

TABLE OF CONTENTS

INTRODUCTION

Have you ever had the feeling that your life has become dominated by activities revolving around working and organizing food, and a typical week consists of waking up in the morning, rushing to work, commuting, working, hasty lunch breaks, commuting home, eating dinner, running errands? Then you may have noticed there's not much time left for anything else. Not to mention the money flowing out of your wallet to satisfy your vegetarian food whims.

Can't resist buying this delicious seitan burger or eating this amazing 5 layer veggie lasagna? The world doesn't end if you do so once in a while. However, if added up, you may quickly realize you are spending too much money on stuff you could easily do without. And not only the financials are important, the ketosis is important too.

As a vegetarian myself, who's been on the Keto diet for some, I clearly understand how difficult is to live like this. That's why I'm here - to help you as much as I can to start this journey, which otherwise would take you great deal of efforts to do it alone. I must admit, I'm not alone in this - my lovely wife follows me in this journey. That motivated me to throw the pans and pots for some time and get to you with as many interesting and delicious recipes as possible.

We may argue that's just the way life is or not, but one thing is for sure - it doesn't take much to make it way better. Planning what to eat, in an organized way, may sound like an impossible task but, in reality, it's more of mental work. What's wrong with eating veggies and cheese? It's great, isn't it?

How much happier would your family, partner, or friends then would be to see you shining? With the constant flow of energy, how much would you develop yourself, having more time to follow a passion or hobby? How much money would there be left in your pocket if you stopped spending it randomly whenever you have a whim?

If you wonder if a conventional cookbook can offer you so much, the answer is simple - NO. Not a conventional one. But this Vegetarian Keto Dietcookbook – oh YES!

What to expect from this cookbook

The pages of this cookbook will be guiding you through the whole process of starting with the Keto diet, how to follow the Keto Diet and do this while still being vegetarian. Diffucult task? Not so much. You will learn how to use different and keto friendly ingredients, get everything ready, and what the actual cooking process looks like.

Furthermore, I will explain how to get on this journey without feeling overwhelmed or unmotivated. Next, you will learn all the pros and cons of the Ketogenic Diet.

Finally, I will present you with plenty of exciting and inspiring keto diet vegetarian recipes, which I love to cook, that will cover all your daily meals and needs, taking you to the extraordinary lifestyle you always dreamed of, without exceeding the consumption of net carbs.

You will also learn plenty of tips that will help you cook your meals in the most efficient way, thus saving lots of time and energy.

I'm so excited to join you in this journey! Are you? Let's get into it!

KETO DIET

Switching to a new diet with the purpose to cleanse your body and burn fat at the same time, can be a tricky process. Most diets require a set of various ingredients, but the ketogenic diet is very specific when it comes to preparing the meals - no carbohydrates, no sugars, no meat, but at the same time lots of fats and proteins. This can prove to be quite difficult for people who aren't prone to spend too much time in the kitchen.

Consuming large amounts of carbohydrates, proteins and fats is nothing to be scared of if you are careful not to eat in excess and you exercise on a regular basis. However, you don't have to be a nutritionist to know that excess of any kind can cause obesity and serious health problems. `Feeding' your body with big amounts of carbohydrates, fats, and protein stimulates the insulin increase, and you become leptin resistant. Moreover, the body weight grows slowly but surely. Uncontrolled diets rich in carbohydrates, fats, and protein can lead to obesity and can increase the risk of heart diseases, cholesterol, high blood pressure, cellular damage and so on.

The ketogenic diet has become extremely popular today, but it is not a new diet at all. In fact, it was created back in the early 1920s by researchers who worked in the Josh Hopkins Medical Center, while they were trying to find a way to decrease the number of seizures in epileptic children. After thorough research, the scientists have discovered that food rich in carbohydrates is actually the main reason why epileptic children have frequent seizures. After the epileptic patients were switched to a ketogenic diet consisting of food rich in fats, proteins and only a little amount of carbohydrates, the number of seizures decreased significantly.

So what exactly happens when you start your ketogenic diet?

This diet's main purpose is to re-shift your body and place the whole 'machinery' on a whole new track. In the Keto diet, the body burns fats much faster than carbohydrates, which is why the meals have to be quite rich in fats. The carbohydrates intake is not prohibited, but you will consume them less. Carbohydrates are the body's main fuel or brain's food (our body turns carbs into glucose). Replacing them with fats makes the body find a substitute source of energy to stay alive. The food poor in carbohydrates basically forces the liver to turn all the fats into fatty acids and ketone bodies. The ketone bodies go straight to the brain and take the place of glucose, giving the brain the needed energy and 'fuel'. High level of ketone bodies in the blood will work not only as a great way for your body to burn all the fats, but it will also decrease the possible risk of seizure, diabetes, cholesterol, lack of energy, depression and many more.

Many people wonder why this diet became such a huge hit among healthy people who only want to lose weight, or cut carbs from their diet even if they have absolutely no traces of epilepsy.

Nutritionists are very vocal about this diet, recommending it as a great way of cleansing your body of toxic substances, eliminating risks of fatal illnesses, losing weight and helping stay fit.

Once you start consuming food based on this diet, your body shifts in a state known as "ketosis". This is a metabolic state where your body takes energy from the ketone bodies created in your blood and not anymore from the sugar that turns into glucose.

You will notice the differences between the ketogenic state and the glycolytic state; the higher the ketone levels in your blood, the more your body will use the fats to burn and turn them into energy. The great thing about this diet is that it will not cause you any weight problems - on the contrary, you will be prone to lose all the fat and excess weight until your body reaches a balanced and healthy fat level. This diet is recommended for life, not only for a couple of weeks until you lose a few kilograms and then return to your old eating habits.

There are people who are afraid it will be too hard for them to get used to life without carbs, but the truth is you will only need several days of low-carb food intake (about 20 grams per day) before feeling the changes. So all these people who swear they couldn't live a day without bread, potatoes, rice, pizza, or noodles, were amazed by the instant weight loss and actually don't want to go back to their old eating habits.

And Yes, this is a diet that requires spending some time in the kitchen. The ketogenic diet does not 'allow' you to eat unhealthy snacks between meals, such as oily potato chips, or chocolate cookies. If you plan to eat unhealthy snacks between meals, then you are going to fail from the start; not only these will pack your body with sugar and other empty calories, but your body may also get confused about the sudden intake of carbs and sugars. So instead of turning towards the fats as its main fuel, it may start using these ingredients as body energy (therefore the process of losing weight will significantly slow down).

The ketogenic diet increases the ketone levels in your body and you can achieve this process either by strictly following the ketogenic diet recipes or by fasting, although for some people this might be a more challenging start.

Most people think that fasting is starving, but it is not. Your keto diet will work perfectly well even if you don't fast, but in case you do want to try this and increase the levels of ketones in your body, then you need to know how fasting works.

Never try to fast for a long time! Always start your fasting with smaller time-frames and make sure you actually eat. People, who want to increase the ketones in their body and try fasting, stick to hour ratios of 18/6 or 19/5. This means that you have five to six hours time-frame in your day when you can eat your food, while the rest of the time you don't eat at all. It is up to you to set the eating hours (based on your daily habits, working hours, weight, the possibility of enduring without food. If you are new to the ketogenic diet, then you can dedicate one day of the week to fasting. As time goes by and you feel stronger to endure a fasting day you can add more days of the weeks.

Consuming meals prepared based on the ketogenic diet will do miracles without fasting as well.

Keto Diet Health Benefits

People who switch to ketogenic diet are not only going to lose weight much easier, but they will also get many benefits along with this way of eating. You will suddenly realize that you are not as hungry as you used to be and this is due to the fact that you are consuming good calories and not empty ones that take your entire energy as it usually happens with sugars and carbohydrates.

Whenever you start a new diet, you usually have to face the ugly side effect called hunger; more often than not, diets cause hunger, which surely leads towards breaking the diet. The reason why this happens is that this type of weight loss diets offer less food, instead of cutting the main culprits that slow down the metabolism. Consuming foods low in carbs will instantly lead towards a lower appetite. You will feel full, even though carbs and sugars will be significantly or completely cut down from your diet. Your body no longer needs them and it feels full of the food rich in proteins, minerals, vitamins, and fats.

A person's body has subcutaneous fat, which is usually stored below the skin and visceral fat, and it is usually found in the abdominal cavity. Visceral fat is the `bad` fat that stores around the organs and consuming it in big amounts can cause insulin resistance, inflammation, and slow metabolism. You don't necessarily have to be overweight to have fat around your organs. This is why this diet is a sure way to cleanse your body, even the parts that are not visible. In general, the ketogenic diet has a great effect when it comes to reducing the abdominal fat that puts you at serious risk of all sorts of diseases, especially type 2 diabetes.

By consuming keto meals, you also lower the level of the triglycerides, as well. These are fat molecules, known for increasing the risk for heart diseases.

The keto diet offers you meals that will help you increase cholesterol levels which ultimately is something good for your body. After all, this is a diet rich in fats; the good cholesterol will remove the bad cholesterol leading it straight to the liver, where the liver will excrete it or reuse it. The more good cholesterol you have in your body, the lower the risk of getting clogged blood vessels or heart attacks.

The keto diet is excellent for people who already have diabetes. Consuming carbs in high amounts surely gives the body energy, but most of it will be turned into glucose, which doesn't work very well for people with diabetes. The glucose goes straight into the bloodstream and raises the sugar levels. Your body will create the hormone insulin, which commands the cells to bring the glucose into the cells; this is when the glucose becomes the body fuel (the glucose is burned or restored in the cells). If you are healthy, this isn't much of a problem. However, if you have diabetes, this can become a life threat. If you are insulin resistant, your cells are not able to detect the insulin, making it hard for the body to bring sugar into the cells. This process is what causes type 2 diabetes. When the body is not capable of secreting insulin to lower the sugar after you consume it, then you will have serious problems with any regular diet that has a significant amount of carbs.

Believe it or not, people who consume ketogenic meals have clearer minds, focus better and feel more energized. It seems that all the energy your body was getting from the glucose was always a poor source (this is why you constantly needed to eat more carbs and sugars to feel full and more energized). Your body can consume much more fats than carbs, so when the fats become the main fuel and are burned at the same time, it seems that they are a never-ending energy source.

What To Eat?

As mentioned before, the ketogenic diet is a diet rich in fats and proteins, and allows just a little percentage of carbohydrates intake, which are the natural component of most fruits and veggies. In general, the keto diet contains high amounts of healthy fats (up to 80 percent) including coconut oil, olive oil, some nuts and seeds. These fats will provide you with energy and will keep you full longer than you might think is possible.

If you wonder whether fats will be the only food in this diet, the answer is NO. Keto meals also offer recipes with all types of non-starchy vegetables. You can eat plenty of broccoli, leafy greens, asparagus, cucumber, and zucchini. In fact, you can use these vegetables to prepare all sorts of foods, not only salads (you can make veggie pizza dough, steam them, eat them raw or combine them as a garnish with your main dish).

The foods you ought to avoid at all costs are noodles, rice, potatoes, processed foods, foods that contain white flour, desserts and other food rich in empty calories that keep you full only for a brief time.

The intake of carbohydrates depends much on your age, weight, gender, and way of life but, in most cases, the keto diet recommends limiting the intake to 20-30 net grams per day. Fats should represent more than 80 percent of your meals, and proteins 15-20 percent.

If you are a beginner, then you can always start with the moderate version of the keto diet, where you are slowly going to cut the carbs from your diet, in case you are afraid that the drastic change of your eating habits can be difficult for you.

TIPS FOR A GREAT START

GO FOR DIVERSITY

That means not repeating the same dish seven times a week. It would be too boring and unhealthy at the same time. Prepare two to three alternatives so you can avoid nutritional burn-out. It may be something as simple as changing the source of proteins (i.e., meat for fish or tofu) or a different type of vegetables.

MAKE A LIST BEFORE SHOPPING

This will train you to stick to the plan, not toss impulse items into your cart. You will save money and time and keep yourself from buying junk food, however crispy it may be. If something's not in your fridge, you will not eat it.

KEEP IT SIMPLE

Although trying more difficult recipes is most welcome, I recommend that you stick to simple recipes at the beginning. Over time, as you become more adept, you may increase the complexity or try your own recipes.

COOK MORE ITEMS AT ONCE, WHENEVER POSSIBLE.

A good example of that would be roasting a couple of things in the oven or on the stove. It's not only time saving, but your electricity bill will look way better.

BUY PRE-CUT VEGETABLES

Even though they may be a bit more expensive, they make your life easier and will save you additional time and efforts.

DRINK LOTS OF WATER

Very often we confuse hunger pangs with dehydration. Water fills your stomach and you do not feel hunger, which is why every diet recommends that you drink plenty of water.

WHAT TO AVOID

- Processed and/or packaged foods like pasta, certain types of cheese, pizzas
- Processed and/or packaged meat
- Vegetable oils
- Soft drinks and sugary beverages
- All kinds of crackers, cookies, cakes, and pastries
- Candy bars
- All kinds of fast foods, including French Fries and Chips

- White bread made of processed white wheat-flour
- Margarine
- Energy drinks
- Ice creams
- MSG and other toxic additives

All things are difficult before they become easy.

Going keto while being vegetarian and maintain a healthy lifestyle in a rushing environment, is pretty damn difficult. That's why I created this book, to offer you my wisdom of not taking the easy way out and eating the junk food tempting you everywhere you go. Instead, to learn to take responsibility for what you eat and what you become as a result.

Given all this, the Keto diet offers one of the best possibilities to eat healthy without losing time and energy cooking every day, even twice a day.

These keto vegetarian recipes are meant to help you initiate the changes and go through the tough beginning. But remember, things seem complicated until you make them easy. The results will be well worth the time. No doubt about it.

This book is an investment that pays huge interests quickly without forcing you to spend a lot of money at the beginning. It's effortless to follow and the results are guaranteed.

Your success is entirely dependent on your determination to stick to the plan and give up on toxic things you considered normal before.

The Keto Vegetarian Recipes in the book are predominantly easy and perfect for beginners. Advanced cooking freaks will find something for themselves as well.

As Buddha said, "to enjoy good health, to bring true happiness to one's family, to bring peace to all, one must first discipline and control one's mind." To take any action, we first need to realize the importance of our diet and how it affects the temples our bodies are. Love the life you have while enjoying the journey to better and healthier nutrition.

SMOOTHIES AND BREAKFAST

Power Green Smoothie

Serves: 2 \ Ready in: 2 minutes

Nutritional Info per serving:

Calories 145, Net Carbs 4.5g Fat 7 g, Protein 15 g

Ingredients:

1 cup Kale, chopped

1 cup Swiss Chard, chopped

1 small Cucumber, chopped

1-inch piece fresh Ginger

1 cup Greek Yogurt, full-fat

1 cup Spinach

4 Ice cubes (optional)

Fresh mint leaves, to decorate

Directions:

- Put all ingredients in a blender, except the ice cubes.
- Blend for 30 seconds, or until desired consistency. If the smoothie is very thick, add water to make it thinner.
- Divide between 2 large glasses.
- Decorate with mint and drink immediately.

Chocolate Cranberry Smoothie Delight

Serves: 2 \ Ready in: 2 minutes

Nutritional Info per serving:

Calories 281, Net Carbs 3.9g Fat 23 g, Protein 12.5 g

Ingredients:

1 cup Coconut milk, chilled

1 oz. Cranberries, frozen

1 scoop whey Chocolate powder

½ cup Heavy cream

1 tsp ground Flaxseed

½ tsp Vanilla extract

2 packets Stevia (optional)

A handful Ice cubes (optional)

2 slices Lime, to decorate

Directions:

- Put all ingredients in a blender, except the ice cubes.
- Blend for 30 seconds, or until desired consistency.
- Divide between 2 large glasses.
- Decorate with the lime slices and serve right away.

Forever Young Smoothie

Serves: 2 \ Ready in: 2 minutes

Nutritional Info per serving:

Calories 190, Net Carbs 3g Fat 15 g, Protein 3 g

Ingredients:

1 Kiwi, peeled and chopped

½ cup Spinach, chopped

⅓ cup Heavy Cream

1 ¼ cups Almond milk, chilled

4 Ice cubes (optional)

Fresh Mint sprigs, to decorate

Directions:

- Put all the ingredients, except the ice cubes, in a blender and whizz until smooth.

- Pour into 2 glasses and garnish with fresh mint. Serve immediately with the ice cubs, if desired.

Almond Butter Shake

Serves: 1 / Preparation Time: 2 minutes

Nutritional Info per serving:

Calories 285, Net Carbs 6.6 g, Fat 20.3 g, Protein 8.9 g

Ingredients:

½ cup Almond Milk

2 tbsp Almond Butter

½ tsp Cinnamon

2 tbsp Flax Meal

15 drops of Stevia

A handful of Ice Cubes, to serve

Directions:

- Add almond butter, flax meal, stevia, cinnamon, and almond milk to a food processor and blend until creamy and smooth.

- If there is trouble blending, add more almond milk.

- Taste and adjust flavor as needed, supplementing a bit of stevia for sweetness or almond butter for creaminess.

- Serve into a serving glass and garnish with additional almond butter, if desired and enjoy!

Watermelon-Avocado Frappé

Serves: 2 \ Ready in: 2 minutes

Nutritional Info per serving:

Calories 410, Net Carbs 6.5 g Fat 35 g, Protein 5 g

Ingredients:

1 Avocado, sliced

1 cup Watermelon, seedless and cubed

1 cup Coconut milk

1 cup baby Spinach

½ cup Heavy cream

1 tsp Chia seeds

Crushed ice cubes

Coconut flakes, unsweetened, to decorate

Directions:

- Put avocado, watermelon cubes, coconut milk, heavy cream, chia seeds, and spinach into a blender.

- Start blending on low speed and increase to high as the ingredients blend until desired consistency.

- Add the ice and stir. Divide between 2 glasses.

- Decorate with the coconut flakes and serve immediately.

Turnip and Leek Tostadas with Eggs

Serves: 4 \ Ready in: 20 minutes

Nutritional Info per serving:

Calories 265, Net Carbs 1.3g, Fat 27,3 g, Protein 9.1 g

Ingredients:

5 Eggs

3 tbsp Olive oil

1 Avocado, pitted, peeled, and sliced

1 large Turnip, shredded

¼ tsp Chili powder

¼ tsp Garlic powder

1 cup Leek, packed

Salt, to taste

Directions:

- Heat one tablespoon of olive oil in a skillet over medium heat. Add the turnip, season with chili, salt, and garlic powder, and cook for about 7 minutes, until tender.

- Place the turnip mixture in a bowl and cool for 5 minutes. Then, crack an egg into the bowl and mix to combine. Heat another tablespoon of oil in the same skillet over medium heat.

- Add ¼ of the turnip mixture in the skillet, flatten with a spatula and cook for about 3 minutes per side. Repeat with the rest of the turnip mixture. Divide the turnip tostadas between 4 plates.

- Grease another skillet with one tablespoon of olive oil and cook the remaining 4 eggs, until the whites become set, about 3 minutes.

- Top the tostadas with leeks, avocado, and a fried egg over the top.

Tofu Scramble with Broccoli Rabe

Serves: 4 \ Ready in: 15 minutes

Nutritional Info per serving:

Calories 334, Net Carbs 4.8 g, Fat 23 g, Protein 7.5 g

Ingredients:

1 (32 oz) package firm Tofu, drained and crumbled

1 pound Broccoli rabe, chopped

3 tbsp Coconut oil

4 tbsp nutritional Yeast

2 tsp sugar-free Soy sauce

½ cup Coconut milk

2 tsp Arrowroot powder

1 tsp Onion powder

1 tsp Garlic powder

½ tsp Sea salt

⅛ tsp Turmeric

4 spring Onions, thinly sliced

Directions:

- Add the broccoli rabe to a pot of boiling water and cook for 5 minutes or until tender but firm; then drain.

- In a mixing bowl add tofu, bok choy, arrowroot powder, onion powder, garlic powder, salt, turmeric, nutritional yeast, and soy sauce.

- Using a fork, lightly crush the mixture.

- Now, heat the coconut oil in a skillet over medium heat.

- Add the tofu mixtute and cook for about 5 minutes, stirring continuously.

- Next, pour the coconut milk over tofu mixture and cook for 1 to 2 minutes until it reaches your desired state of creaminess.

- Serve immediately sprinkled with fresh spring onions.

Tip: *Sprinkle some of your favorite cheese for creamier taste.*

Zucchini Pancakes

Serves: 2 pancakes \ Ready in: 15 minutes

Nutritional Info per serving:

Calories 312, Net Carbs 4.8 g, Fat 23 g, Protein 7.5 g

Ingredients:

⅓ cup Coconut flour

1 cup Zucchini grated

½ cup Almond milk, unsweetened

1 Egg, slightly beaten

½ tsp ground Nutmeg

1 tbsp Coconut oil, melted

1 tsp grated Parmesan cheese

Kosher salt, to taste

Fresh Parsley, chopped to serve

Directions:

1. Dry pat the zucchini with a paper towel to remove moisture, and set aside.
1. Mix together the flour along with salt, nutmeg and Parmesan cheese, into a bowl. In a separate bowl, mix the egg, milk, and coconut oil.
2. Gradually pour the wet mixture into the bowl with the dry ingredients, whisking to combine. Stir in the zucchinis.
3. Heat a skillet over medium heat and grease with cooking spray.
4. Add ½ of the mixture and cook for 2 to 3 minutes per side, until golden.
5. Repeat with the rest of the batter.
6. Serve immediately sprinkled with fresh parsley.

Tip: *Serve with yogurt sauce for creamier and richer taste.*

Green Frittata Muffins

Serves: 4 \ Ready in: 25 minutes

Nutritional Info per serving:

Calories 367, Net Carbs 2.5 g, Fat 28.7 g, Protein 24 g

Ingredients:

1 Zucchini, shredded

1 handful Kale, chopped

½ cup Green Beans

8 Eggs

1 Garlic clove, crushed

1 cup Cheddar cheese, finely grated

1 tbsp Olive oil

Salt and ground Black pepper, to taste

Directions:

- Preheat your oven to 425 degrees F. Grease 8 muffin trays and set aside.

- Meanwhile, heat the olive oil in a skillet over medium heat. Add the zucchini and green beans, and cook for about 5 minutes. Remove from the heat and stir in the kale.

- In a large bowl beat the eggs and add the cooked vegetables and cheese. Gently stir to combine well.

- Divide the mixture evenly between the prepared muffin trays.

- Bake for 15 mins, until the frittatas are set and golden.

- Remove from the oven and leave to cool slightly, before serving.

Buffalo Cheese Egg Muffins

Serves: 6 (12 muffins) \ Ready in: 35 minutes

Nutritional Info per serving:

Calories 213, Net Carbs 8 g, Fat 4.8 g, Protein 15.3 g

Ingredients:

1 lb. Asparagus stalks, halved and ends trimmed

6 Eggs, beaten

3 cups grape Tomatoes, chopped

¼ cup Basil

1 tbsp Olive oil

¾ cup shredded buffalo cheese

Salt and ground Black pepper, to taste

Cooking spray

Directions:

- Preheat the oven to 375 degrees F. Spray 12 muffin tins with cooking spray.
- Heat the olive oil in a skillet over medium heat.
- Add the asparagus stalks, and cook for 5 minutes until tender.
- Fill the muffin tins halfway with asparagus.
- Place basil and tomatoes on top of each tin and season with salt and black pepper.
- Top with buffalo cheese.
- Pour the eggs over, filling the tins ¾ to the top.
- Place in the oven and bake for 25 minutes.
- Serve with crunchy salad.

Breakfast Hash with Swiss Chard

Serves: 2 \ Ready in: 25 minutes

Nutritional Info per serving:

Calories 245, Net Carbs 5.2 g, Fat 16.2 g, Protein 7.3 g

Ingredients:

4 Swiss Chard, chopped

1 Turnip, shredded

1 Bell pepper, chopped

¼ tsp Cumin

¼ tsp Chili Paprika

⅛ tsp Salt

½ Onion, chopped

⅛ tsp ground Black pepper

2 large Eggs

2 tbsp Olive oil

Directions:

- Heat 1 tablespoon of olive oil in a skillet over medium heat. Add the bell peppers, onions, turnips, paprika, cumin, salt, and pepper.

- Cook for 8 minutes, stirring occasionally, or until the vegetables are tender.

- Stir in swiss chard and cook for another 2 minutes. Transfer to a bowl and set aside.

- In the same skillet, add the remaining olive oil. Crack the eggs and cook until set. Season to taste with salt and pepper.

- Divide the hash veggie mixture between two plates and top with a fried egg.

Breakfast Bowl the Mexican Way

Serves: 4 \ Ready in: 15 minutes

Nutritional Info per serving:

Calories 280, Ner Carbs g,4.2 Fat 20.5 g, Protein 14.1 g

Ingredients:

2 tbsp chopped Cilantro

½ tsp Garlic powder

1 Avocado, mashed

8 Eggs, beaten

¾ cup Tomatoes, chopped

1 tbsp Olive oil

¼ tsp Paprika

½ cup Green Beans

1 cup Turnip, chopped

¼ cup Onion, chopped

1 tsp Jalapeño, minced

¼ tsp Chili powder

Juice of ½ Lime

Cooking spray

Directions:

- Heat the olive oil in a skillet over medium heat. Add the chopped turnip, chili powder, paprika, and garlic powder. Cover the skillet with a lid and cook for 7 minutes.

- Meanwhile, combine the green beans, avocado, onion, jalapeno, lime juice, and cilantro in a bowl. Transfer the cooked turnip to a separate bowl.

- In the same skillet add oil if necessary and pour the eggs, stir to scramble, and cook for a couple of minutes until set.

- Place the eggs on top of the turnip noodles, and top with the avocado/beans mixture. Serve immediately.

Scrambled Eggs with Mozzarella and Peppers

Serves: 2 \ Ready in: 12 minutes

Nutritional Info per serving:

Calories 305, Net Carbs 4.3 g, Fat 13.4 g, Protein 16.6 g

Ingredients:

4 Eggs, beaten

½ small Onion, finely chopped

3 tbsp Mozzarella cheese, shredded

½ tbsp Olive oil

1 medium red Bell pepper, diced

¼ Avocado, cubed

1 tbsp fresh Basil, chopped

Salt and ground Black pepper, to taste

Directions:

- Heat the olive oil in a skillet over medium heat. Add the bell pepper and onion and cook for about 5 minutes until softened. Add the avocado and season with salt and pepper to taste.

- Pour the beaten eggs over the vegetables, stir constantly and cook until the eggs are set but still moist and tender, for about 5 minutes.

- Finally, stir in the Mozzarella cheese and fresh basil. Serve with green salad.

Breakfast Granola

Serves: 8 \ Ready in: 60 minutes

Nutritional Info per serving:

Calories 260, Net Carbs 3.8 g, Fat 24.2 g, Protein 6.2g

Ingredients:

2 tbsp Coconut oil, melted

2 tbsp unsweetened Coconut, shredded

2 tbsp granulated Erythritol

¼ tsp ground Cinnamon

¼ cup Pumpkin seeds

¼ cup Sunflower seeds

1 tsp Vanilla extract

1 teaspoon Nutmeg, freshly grated

½ cup Walnuts, chopped

½ cup Hazelnuts, crushed

½ cup Almonds, slivered

Directions:

- In a large bowl, whisk together 1 tablespoon of the coconut oil, vanilla, sunflower seeds, pumpkin seeds, shredded coconut, hazelnuts, almonds, walnuts, erythritol, and cinnamon, and stir to combine.

- Preheat your oven to 320 degrees F. Lightly grease a baking sheet with the remaining coconut oil. Spread the mixture out in an even layer onto the baking sheet.

- Bake for 40-50 minutes, until the granola is crispy. Leave to cool before serving time.

Tip: *Serve over yogurt or ice cream for a delicious dessert.*

Keto Bagels with Mascarpone Cheese

Serves: 3 \ Ready in: 30 minutes

Nutritional Info per serving:

Calories 281 , Net Carbs 3.1 g, Fat 17.8 g, Protein 26.5 g

Ingredients:

1 cup Almond flour

2 large Eggs

2 cups Mozzarella cheese, shredded

¼ cup Mascarpone cheese

1 tbsp Olive oil

1 tsp Poppy seeds

1 tsp Onion powder

¼ tsp Black pepper

1 tbsp Baking powder

½ tsp Salt

1 tsp Sesame seeds

1 tsp Garlic powder

2 tbsp Coconut oil

Directions:

- Preheat the oven to 400 F and grease a donut pan with coconut oil.

- In the meantime, add the Mozzarella cheese and mascarpone to a microwave-safe bowl and microwave on high until the cheese is melted, about 2 minutes.

- In a mixing bowl lightly beat the eggs just until blended. Season with salt and pepper.

- Add the flour, baking powder and oil to the eggs and mix until everything is well incorporated. Add the cheese mixture and stir to combine well. Pour the mixture into the donut pan.

- In a small bowl, combine the poppy seeds, onion powder, garlic powder, and sesame seeds. Sprinkle the top of each bagel with the mixture.

- Place in the preheated oven and bake for 15-20 minutes, or until golden brown.

- Cool on a wire rack for 4 to 5 minutes before serving warm with cream cheese and tomato slices (optional).

Greek-Style Omelet with Cherry Tomatoes

Serves: 4 / Preparation Time: 40 minutes

Nutritional Info per serving:

Calories 411, Net Carbs 4.1 g, Fat 32.5 g, Protein 23.6 g

Ingredients:

5 ounces Spinach

8 ounces crumbled Feta cheese

1 pint halved Cherry Tomatoes

10 Eggs

3 tbsp Olive Oil

4 Scallions, diced

Directions:

* Preheat your oven to 350 degrees F. Drizzle the oil in a 2-quart casserole and place in the oven until heated. In a bowl, whisk the eggs along with the pepper and salt.

* Stir in the rest of the ingredients. Pour the mixture in the casserole and place back in the oven. Bake for 25 minutes.

Herbed Buttered Eggs

Serves: 2 / Preparation Time: 15 minutes

Nutritional Info per serving:

Calories 268, Net Carbs 1.5 g, Fat 23.5 g, Protein 12.8 g

Ingredients:

1 tbsp Coconut Oil

2 tbsp Butter

1 tsp fresh Thyme

4 Eggs

2 Garlic Cloves, minced

½ cup chopped Parsley

½ cup chopped Cilantro

¼ tsp Cayenne Pepper

Directions:

- Melt the butter and coconut oil together in a skillet over medium heat.
- Add garlic and cook for 30 seconds. Add thyme and cook for 30 more seconds. Stir in parsley and cilantro and cook for about 1-2 minutes, until crisp.
- Crack the eggs into the skillet. Lower the heat and cook for 4-6 minutes.
- Serve seasoned with cayenne pepper and salt if desired.

Italian Caprese Frittata

Serves: 1 / Preparation Time: 15 minutes

Nutritional Info per serving:

Calories 305, Net Carbs 4.6 g, Fat 18.5 g, Protein 30.6 g

Ingredients:

2 Eggs

6 Basil Leaves

2 ounces fresh Mozzarella, sliced

1 tbsp Butter

1 tbsp Water

1 Tomato, sliced

Salt and Pepper, to taste

Directions:

- Whisk the eggs along with the water, and season with some salt and pepper.
- Melt the butter in a skillet and cook the eggs for 30 seconds.
- Arrange the sliced tomato and Mozzarella on top of the eggs.
- Cook for about 2 minutes. Cover the skillet and cook for 1 more minute.
- Top with basil leaves and serve immediately.

LUNCH

Arugula Salad with Walnuts

Serves: 4 \ Ready in: 10 minutes

Nutritional Info per serving:

Calories 228, Net Carbs 2.1 g, Fat 22.1 g, Protein 8.4 g

Ingredients:

6 cups baby Arugula

2 large Eggs

½ cup Blue cheese

3 tbsp Walnut oil

½ tsp Dijon mustard

¼ cup Walnuts, chopped

2 tbsp Lime juice

⅓ cup fresh Cilantro, minced

Sea Salt to taste

Directions:

- Cook the eggs in a pot of boiling salted water over medium heat for 6 minutes, then remove to a bowl of ice-cold water to cool.

- Meanwhile, gently combine baby arugula, walnuts, and cilantro in a bowl.

- For the dressing, combine the lime juice, mustard, and salt. Gradually whisk in the oil to make a creamy dressing.

- Once the eggs cooled, peel and cut into quarters.

- Arrange the salad on a serving platter. Place the eggs on top and crumble over the blue cheese. Drizzle with the dressing right before serving.

Spinach Salad with Olives & Cashews

Serves: 4 \ Ready in: 25 minutes

Nutritional Info per serving:

Calories 175, Net Carbs 5.1 g, Fat 13.1 g, Protein 5.3 g

Ingredients:

1 tbsp Olive oil, divided

1 medium head Cauliflower, cut into individual florets

3 cups baby Spinach leaves

12 black Olives, pitted, roughly chopped

¼ cup raw Cashews

½ tsp Dijon mustard

½ tbsp Lemon juice

¼ cup Almond milk

1 Garlic clove, minced

Salt and ground Black pepper, to taste

Directions:

- Preheat the oven to 400 F and line a baking dish with parchment paper.
- Place the cauliflower florets onto the baking dish, drizzle with the olive oil and toss well. Sprinkle with a little salt and ground black pepper. Bake for 20 minutes until golden and crispy on the ends. Leave to cool.
- Meanwhile, blend the cashews, almond milk, garlic, mustard, lemon juice, salt and pepper in a food processor until smooth.
- Transfer the cooled cauliflower to a large serving bowl and mix with the baby spinach leaves and black olives.
- Pour the dressing over and serve right away.

Spanish-Style Tortilla with Zucchini

Serves: 4 \ Ready in: 15 minutes

Nutritional Info per serving:

Calories 220, Net Carbs 2.3 g, Fat 16.7 g, Protein 13.5 g

Ingredients:

1 Zucchini, peeled and chopped

1 Onion, chopped

8 large Eggs

2 tbsp Olive oil

2 Tomatoes, sliced

Salt and pepper, to taste

Directions:

- Heat the oil in a skillet over medium heat and add the onion. Reduce the heat to low and cook until the onion until soft and caramelized, but not burned, about 4-7 minutes.

- Add the zucchini and cook with the onion for another 15 minutes.

- Meanwhile, in a large bowl lightly beat the eggs with a fork.

- Once the onion and zucchini are cooked, remove the skillet from the heat and carefully tip them into the eggs. Season to taste with salt and pepper.

- Return the mixture to the skillet, add some more oil if needed and cook for 10 minutes on low heat, until is set and the edges are golden.

- Flip on a dish and slide back into the skillet and cook for 2-3 more minutes, or until golden and cooked through. Cut into wedges before serving.

- Serve hot or cold with tomato salad.

Roasted Zucchini with Garlicky Yogurt

Serves: 4 \ Ready in: 25 minutes

Nutritional Info per serving:

Calories 191, Net Carbs 3.2 g, Fat 12.4 g, Protein 8.8 g

Ingredients:

2 large Zucchinis, sliced into ¼ inch pieces

2 cups full-fat Yogurt

2 Garlic cloves, minced

2 tbsp Olive oil + 1 tsp to serve

2 tbsp fresh Dill, finely chopped

Kosher salt, to taste

Directions:

- Preheat the oven to 400 degrees F.
- Grease a large roasting tray with olive oil and set aside.
- Press onto the zucchini pieces with a paper towel to squeeze out excess water.
- Arrange them on a prepared greased tray and season with salt.
- Place the tray in the oven and bake for 20-25 minutes until golden.
- Meanwhile, in a bowl mix together the yogurt, garlic, and dill.
- Season to taste with salt and let cool in the fridge until ready to serve.
- Transfer the zucchini to a serving platter.
- Pour the garlic yogurt over the top, drizzle with olive oil and serve.

Bell Pepper and Artichoke Antipasto

Serves: 4 \ Ready in: 25 minutes

Nutritional Info per serving:

Calories 107, Net Carbs 3.9 g, Fat 6.1 g, Protein 5.8 g

Ingredients:

2 Bell peppers, seeds removed, sliced

1 ¼ tsp dried Oregano

1 ½ cups canned Artichoke hearts, quartered

1 tsp Olive oil

¼ cup Provolone cheese, cubed

½ cup halved Kalamata black olives

4 cups mixed Greens

1 tbsp fresh Basil, cut into thin strips

Salt and ground Black pepper, to taste

Directions:

- Preheat your oven to 450 degrees F and line two baking sheets with waxed paper.

- Place the bell peppers on one sheet and sprinkle with half the oregano. Season with salt and pepper.

- Arrange the artichokes on the other sheet, drizzle with the olive oil and sprinkle with the rest of the oregano, as well as some salt and pepper.

- Bake them for 20 minutes.

- Place the roasted peppers and artichokes in a large bowl and stir in the provolone cheese and olives.

- Serve antipasto at room temperature over the mixed greens topped with the fresh basil.

Carrot Noodle Cheddar Soup with Leeks

Serves: 4 \ Ready in: 20 minutes

Nutritional Info per serving:

Calories 323, Net Carbs 6.7 g, Fat 20.2 g, Protein 17.3 g

Ingredients:

2 tbsp Olive oil

1 Onion, chopped

1 large Carrot, peeled, spiralized

6 cups Vegetable broth

1 cup Cheddar cheese, grated

3 Garlic cloves, minced

2 Leeks, thinly sliced

2 Celery stalks, diced

1 Bay leaf

4 Thyme sprigs

1 Rosemary sprig, chopped

2 tbsp Hives, minced, to garnish

Salt and Black pepper, to taste

Directions:

- To start, heat the oil in a large pot over medium heat.
- Add the onion, leeks, celery, and garlic, and cook the vegetables until they are aromatic and just tender, about 5 minutes.
- Add 1 cup of water, vegetable broth, bay leaf, thyme, and rosemary, and bring the mixture to a boil.
- Reduce the heat to low, add the carrots, and cook until tender, about 7-8 minutes.
- Discard the bay leaf. Taste, adjust the seasonings, and scatter with the chives.
- Divide into bowls and serve hot, topped with grated Cheddar cheese.

Tofu Green Curry

Serves: 4 \ Ready in: 25 minutes

Nutritional Info per serving:

Calories 268, Net Carbs 3.5 g, Fat 17.6 g, Protein 14.5 g

Ingredients:

14 oz extra-firm Tofu, drained and cut into 1-inch cubes

1 Kohlrabi, peeled and cut into 1-inch cubes

1 tbsp Coconut oil

1 tbsp sugar-free Soy sauce

2 tbsp green Curry paste

28 oz (2 cans) Coconut milk

2 cups Broccoli florets

½ cup fresh Cilantro, minced

Juice from 1 Lime

1 Avocado, sliced

Directions:

- Heat coconut oil in a saucepan over moderate heat. Add the tofu and soy sauce and cook for 10, stirring gently to coat the pieces without breaking them, until golden brown.

- Using a slotted spoon transfer them to a bowl. Set aside

- In the same saucepan, combine the coconut milk, curry paste, kohlrabi and bring to a boil. Lower the heat and cook until tender, 6 to 9 minutes.

- Stir broccoli and tofu with the kohlrabi and cook until broccoli is bright green, about 5 minutes. Remove from the heat and add in lime juice and cilantro.

- Top with avocado slices and serve.

Authentic Gazpacho Andaluz

Serves: 4 \ Ready in: 2h 15 minutes

Nutritional Info per serving:

Calories 235, Net Carbs 2.8 g, Fat 16.9 g, Protein 6.5 g

Ingredients:

8 Tomatoes, peeled

½ Cucumber, peeled and seeds scooped out

½ Green pepper, chopped

½ red pepper, chopped

½ Onion, chopped

2 Garlic cloves, peeled and chopped

¼ cup Olive oil

2 tbsp wine vinegar

Salt and pepper, to taste

1 cup diced Onion, Red pepper, Green pepper, to garnish

2 hard-boiled Eggs, cut into chunks, to garnish

Directions:

- In a food processor mix together the tomatoes, oil and vinegar.

- Add the vegetables and garlic, and blend until uniform and smooth.

- Season to taste with salt and black pepper. If it is too thick, add some water and stir to combine.

- Pass the gazpacho through a strainer and pour into a bowl, cover with plastic wrap, and chill at least 2 hours.

- Serve the gazpacho in individual cups garnished with onion, red pepper, green pepper, and hard-boiled eggs.

Simple Thyme-Flavored Beet Risotto

Serves: 2 \ Ready in: 15 minutes

Nutritional Info per serving:

Calories 245, Net Carbs 4.3 g, Fat 22 g, Protein 9 g

Ingredients:

2 large Beets, peeled and cubed

⅓ cup chopped Walnuts

¼ cup Vegetable broth

2 tbsp minced Shallots

1 tbsp Olive oil

1 Garlic cloves, pressed

¼ cup Parmesan cheese, grated

1 tsp Thyme leaves

Salt and Black pepper, to taste

Directions:

- Place the beet cubes in your food processor and pulse until rice is formed.
- Warm the olive oil in a skillet over medium heat and cook the garlic and shallots until soft, about 2-3 minutes. Stir in the beet rice, thyme and broth.
- Bring the mixture to a boil, reduce the heat, and cook covered, until the beet rice is fluffy and tender, 5-6 minutes.
- Taste and adjust the seasonings. Stir in the Parmesan cheese.
- Serve topped with walnuts.

Tip: *Garnish with diced avocado and poached eggs for the perfect lunch.*

Green Beans with Turnip Rice

Serves: 4 \ Ready in: 3 hours and 25 minutes

Nutritional Info per serving:

Calories 214, Net Carbs 6.1 g, Fat 10.9 g, Protein 11.2 g

Ingredients:

1 lb. Green Beans

3 large Turnips, cubed

2 Eggs, beaten

1 small Onion, diced

4 Scallions, diced

1 tbsp Tamari sauce

½ tbsp Olive oil

Salt and White pepper, to taste

½ cup grated Parmesan cheese

Cooking spray

Directions:

- Pulse the turnips in a food processor and process until the pieces are about the size of a grain of rice.

- Coat a skillet with cooking spray, place over medium heat, add the eggs, scramble and cook until set. Transfer to a plate and set aside.

- In the same skillet, warm the olive oil and cook the onion until translucent, 3 minutes. Add the rice and green beans, and cook for 5 more minutes.

- Stir in the riced turnip, green beans, salt, and white pepper. Cover with a lid and cook until the turnip is fluffy and tender, about 4 minutes.Stir in the scrambled eggs and scallions. Serve warm topped with Parmesan cheese.

Tip: *For an easy vegetarian dinner serve garnished with some diced avocado and poached eggs*

Garlicky Squash Risotto with Leeks

Serves: 2 \ Ready in: 40 minutes

Nutritional Info per serving:

Calories 182, Net Carbs 6.2 g, Fat 10.6 g, Protein 7.5 g

Ingredients:

⅓ cup Grana Padano cheese, grated

1 medium Butternut squash, cubed

1 cup sliced Leeks

½ cup Vegetable broth

1 Garlic clove, pressed

A pinch of Thyme

1 tbsp Butter

Salt and ground Black pepper, to taste

Cilantro, to garnish

Directions:

- Place the squash cubes in your food processor and pulse a few times until you get a rice-like size and consistency.

- Heat the butter in a skillet over medium heat and cook the leeks for 3 minutes until tender. Add the garlic and sauté until fragrant, about 30 seconds.

- Stir in the squash rice and thyme, and cook until al-dente and heated through, about 2 minutes.

- Pour the broth over and bring the mixture to a simmer. Cook for 10 minutes on low heat before adding the salt and pepper.

- Stir in Grana Padano until the cheese is melted.

- Spread on a plate and top with coriander.

Butternut Squash Soup

Serves: 6 \ Ready in: 45

Nutritional Info per serving:

Calories 204, Net Carbs 5.3 g, Fat 17.1 g, Protein 12.8 g

Ingredients:

1 yellow Onion, chopped

2 tbsp Olive oil, divided

1 stalk Celery, chopped

1 Garlic clove, pressed

2 ½ cups Butternut squash, peeled and cubed

2 cups Vegetable broth

¾ cups Carrots, peeled and diced

¾ cup Coconut milk, plus more for garnish

¼ cup Pepitas, toasted

Salt and freshly ground Black pepper, to taste

¼ cup Cilantro leaves, to serve

Directions:

- Heat the oil in a large saucepan. Cook and stir the onion, carrots, and celery in hot oil until lightly browned, 5 to 6 minutes. Add the butternut squash, garlic, salt and pepper, and continue to cook for another 2-3 minutes.

- Pour the vegetable broth and bring the mixture to a boil. Turn the heat to medium-high, cover with a lid and cook for about 25 minutes, until the squash is completely tender.

- Transfer the soup in a blender and pulse until smooth. Add the coconut milk and stir with a whisk until the color of the soup is consistent. Taste and adjust the seasonings.

- Divide the soup between bowls and garnish with coconut milk, pepitas and cilantro leaves to serve.

Tip: *To convert this meal into a curried butternut squash soup add one teaspoon of curry powder.*

Mushroom-Bell Pepper Pizza

Serves: 2 \ Ready in: 25 minutes

Nutritional Info per serving:

Calories 278, Net Carbs 1.8 g, Fat 16.6 g, Protein 32.2 g

Ingredients:

Pizza Base:

½ cup Almond flour

2 tbsp psyllium Husk

2 tbsp cream cheese

2 tbsp Parmesan cheese, fresh

1 ½ cup Mozzarella cheese

1 tbsp Olive oil

1 egg

Kosher salt and pepper, to taste

Toppings:

1 cup shredded Cheddar cheese

1 Tomato, sliced

1 tsp Italian seasoning

¼ cup sugar-free Tomato Sauce

½ cup Portobello Mushrooms, sliced

¼ medium Bell pepper, thinly sliced

4 black olives

1 tsp dried Oregano

Fresh Basil, for topping

Directions:

- Preheat oven to 390 F. Grease a baking sheet with olive oil and set aside.

- Meanwhile, melt the Mozzarella cheese for 40-50 seconds in the microwave.

- In a separate bowl, combine the dry ingredients and add the egg. Mix together a little bit. Add the melted Mozzarella cheese and cream cheese and mix well.

- On a lightly floured surface, using a rolling pin, flatten the dough, and form a circle.Transfer the dough to the prepared baking sheet. Bake for 10 minutes, then remove from the oven.

- Top the pizza with the toppings except for the basil and olives, and bake for another 8-10 minutes.

- Remove pizza from the oven, turn off the oven and top with the basil and olives.

Cheddar-Broccoli Tart

Serves: 4 \ Ready in: 20 minutes

Nutritional Info per serving:

Calories 289, Net Carbs 2.3 g, Fat 21.6 g, Protein 20.2 g

Ingredients:

8 Eggs

1 cup Cheddar cheese, grated

1 Garlic clove, crushed

½ Broccoli head, trimmed and cut into florets

Salt and pepper, to taste

Cooking spray

¼ cup sour cream, to garnish

Salad leaves, to garnish

Directions:

- Preheat the oven to 350 degrees F. Grease a round baking dish with cooking spray.

- Beat the eggs in a large bowl using a fork, then add the garlic and whisk again. Season to taste with salt and pepper.

- Pour the mixture into the baking dish.

- Lay the broccoli florets onto the eggs in one tidy row.

- Sprinkle with the grated cheese on top. Bake for 15 minutes until cooked through and golden.

- Slice the tart into wedges and serve with the sour cream and salad leaves.

Saffron Veggie Paella with Carrot Rice

Serves: 4 \ Ready in: 20 minutes

Nutritional Info per serving:

Calories 190, Net Carbs 6.9 g, Fat 7.5 g, Protein 8.5 g

Ingredients:

3 large Carrots, shredded

1 red Bell pepper, cut into long strips

14 ounces canned Tomatoes

1 Onion, diced

½ tsp Cayenne pepper

2 cups Broccoli florets

1 cup Green Beans

14 oz Artichoke hearts, quartered

1 tsp Saffron threads

1 tbsp Olive oil

2 Garlic cloves, minced

1 ½ tsp smoked Paprika

1 tbsp Cilantro, chopped

¼ cup dry White wine

½ cup Kalamata olives, sliced

½ cup Veggie broth

1 handful Parsley, roughly chopped

1 lemon, cut in wedges

Sea salt and Black pepper, to taste

Directions:

- Place the grated carrot in the food processor and pulse until rice is formed.
- Heat the olive oil in a skillet and cook the onion, garlic for 3 minutes, or until fragrant. Stir in cayenne pepper, saffron, salt and paprika.
- Add the bell pepper and broccoli, and cook for 3 minutes. Stir in the rest of the ingredients and cook for 10 minutes.
- Taste, adjust the seasonings, and scatter with the parsley.
- Serve warm with the lemon wedges.

One-Pot Thai Vegetable Curry

Serves: 3 \ Ready in: 30 minutes

Nutritional Info per serving:

Calories 220, Net Carbs 2.7 g, Fat 19.2 g, Protein 3.1 g

Ingredients:

2 Carrots, peeled and chopped

¾ cup Coconut milk

1 tbsp Olive oil

1 small Onion, chopped

½ tbsp fresh Ginger, peeled and minced

1 Garlic clove, pressed

1 red Bell pepper, sliced

1 orange Bell pepper, sliced

½ cup Kale leaves, chopped

¼ cup Water

1 tbsp Thai red Curry paste

Salt and Black pepper, to taste

Directions:

- Heat oil in a saucepan over moderate heat. Cook and stir onion until soft, about 3 minutes.

- Add garlic and ginger to the saucepan and continue cooking until fragrant, about 30 seconds.

- Add the carrots and peppers and cook until the peppers are tender, about 4 minutes, stirring occasionally.

- Add the kale, coconut milk, water, and curry paste to the vegetable mixture and cook until the color of the sauce is consistent.

- Cover and bring to a simmer, then continue to cook for 5-6 minutes over medium-low heat.

- Once the cooking is complete, remove the saucepan from the heat. Taste and adjust the seasonings.

Tip: *If you add raw tofu, it will soak up most of the liquid, and baking it vastly improves the texture.*

Chard and Green Beans Soup with Parmesan

Serves: 4 \ Ready in: 18 minutes

Nutritional Info per serving:

Calories 233, Net Carbs 6.1 g, Fat 13.5 g, Protein 14.9 g

Ingredients:

6 cups chard, chopped

2 tbsp Olive oil

6 cups Veggie broth

1 Celery stalk, 5-inch long, diced

1 Carrot, chopped

1 oz Parmesan cheese, finely grated

1 lb. Green Beans

2 Garlic cloves, minced

¾ cup white Onion, finely chopped

2 tbsp Thyme, chopped

¼ tsp red pepper flakes

Salt and ground Black pepper, to taste

4 tbsp Parmesan cheese, grated for garnishing

Directions:

- In a large saucepan over medium heat, heat the oil. Cook the garlic, onions and celery, and stir gently in hot oil, until tender, for about 2-3 minutes.

- Pour in the veggie broth and stir in the red pepper flakes and thyme. Bring the mixture to a boil.

- Reduce the heat to medium-low, add the carrot, chard, and green beans.

- Cook until fork-tender, 7-8 minutes.

- Season with salt and pepper to taste.

- Divide the soup between bowls and serve with the Parmesan cheese on top of each bowlful.

Yummy Spring Vegetable Soup

Serves: 4 \ Ready in: 15 minutes

Nutritional Info per serving:

Calories 175, Net Carbs 3.7 g, Fat 10.5 g, Protein 9.3 g

Ingredients:

1 Onion, finely chopped

1 Garlic clove, minced

2 tbsp Olive oil

4 cups Vegetable broth

½ lb Asparagus, ends trimmed and chopped

¾ cup Green Beans

1 cup Spinach, chopped

2 tbsp fresh Mint leaves, finely chopped

2 spring Onions, sliced

¼ cup Parmesan cheese, finely grated

Salt and pepper, to taste

Extra virgin Olive oil, to garnish

Directions:

- Heat the oil in a saucepan over medium heat, add the onion and garlic, and cook until tender, about 3 minutes.
- Pour in the broth and bring to a boil.
- Reduce the heat to low and add the asparagus, green beans and cook for a further 10 minutes.
- Season to taste with salt and pepper.
- Remove the soup from the heat, add the spinach and mint and stir to combine.
- Divide between 4 soup bowls.
- Top with the spring onions and Parmesan cheese.

Tip: *Drizzle with extra virgin olive oil, if desired and serve.*

Pesto Soup with Zucchini Noodles

Serves: 4 \ Ready in: 15 minutes

Nutritional Info per serving:

Calories 154, Net Carbs 3.2 g, Fat 10.5 g, Protein 10.1 g

Ingredients:

2 Zucchinis, spiralized

1 Carrot, chopped

2 Celery stalks, diced

6 cups Vegetable broth

2 Garlic cloves, minced

1 red Onion, finely chopped

1 tbsp Olive oil

Pesto:

1 tbsp Olive Oil

1 Garlic Clove, minced

1 tbsp Pine nuts

1 cup Basil, packed

2 tbsp grated Parmesan Cheese

Salt and Pepper, to taste

Directions:

- Heat the olive oil in a large pot. Add onions and celery, and cook until soft, about 3 minutes. Add garlic and cook for 30 more seconds, or until fragrant.

- Pour in the broth and bring the mixture to a boil. Add carrots and cook for another 3 minutes. Reduce the heat to low, add the zucchini noodles, and cook for 5 minutes.

- Meanwhile, place all of the pesto ingredients in a food processor, and process until smooth.

- Serve the soup in bowls, float a little pesto in the middle.

Tip: *Some suggestions for different toppings include tofu, baby bok choy, bean sprouts, and cabbage.*

Veggie Vegan Soup with Chillies

Serves: 6 \ Ready in: 20 minutes

Nutritional Info per serving:

Calories 127, Net Carbs 3.9 g, Fat 6.5 g, Protein 6.6 g

Ingredients:

1 cup Celery, diced	1 pinch dried Thyme
3 Garlic cloves, minced	2 red Chilis, finely chopped
2 tbsp Olive oil	1 baby Eggplant, chopped
1 cup Carrots, sliced	½ tsp dried Oregano
3 Zucchinis, chopped	1 cup Onion, diced
4 Tomatoes, chopped	Salt and Pepper, to taste
4 cups Veggie broth	Fresh Cilantro, chopped to serve
½ tsp dried Basil	

Directions:

- Heat the olive oil in a saucepan over medium heat. Add celery, onion and garlic, and cook for 3-4 minutes until soft.

- Stir in the chilli and dried spices, cook for another minute and season with salt end pepper.

- Stir in the eggplant along with the carrots, chopped tomatoes, broth, oregano, thyme, and basil.

- Bring the mixture to a boil, reduce the heat and let simmer for 10 minutes.

- Stir in the zoodles and cook for 5 more minutes, stirring occasionally.

- Taste, adjust the seasonings and serve warm over cauliflower rice, sprinkled with fresh cilantro.

Scrambled Eggs with Arugula Pesto

Serves: 4 \ Ready in: 15 minutes

Nutritional Info per serving:

Calories 575, Net Carbs 5.2 g, Fat 52.5 g, Protein 20.1 g

Ingredients:

8 Eggs

¼ cup Coconut milk

2 tablespoons Olive oil

Salt and ground Black pepper, to taste

For the Arugula Pesto:

2 cups Arugula

1 Garlic clove, pressed

1 cup Parmesan cheese, grated

½ cup Olive oil

½ cup Almonds, blanched

1 tbsp fresh Lime juice

Directions:

- To make the pesto, put the Parmesan cheese in a food processor, add the garlic, and tip in the almonds, lime juice, and the oil. Blend until you obtain the desired consistency. Set aside.

- Now, heat the olive oil in a sauté pan over medium heat.

- In a bowl beat the eggs with a fork. Stir in milk. Season to taste with salt and pepper. Pour the mixture into the pan and cook for 6-7 minutes, gently stirring, until the eggs are set but tender.

- Serve the scrambled eggs topped with the pesto.

Zucchini and Broccoli Keto Pizza

Serves: 4 \ Ready in: 30 minutes

Nutritional Info per serving:

Calories 180, Net Carbs 6.2g, Fat 8.5 g, Protein 14.6 g

Ingredients:

1 pound Broccoli, broken into florets

2 cups Almond flour

2 cups Greek-style yogurt

½ cup Mozzarella cheese

1 cup tomato puree, sugar-free

¼ cup Black Olives, pitted and sliced

2 tsp Olive oil

1 tbsp dry Oregano

1 Zucchini, peeled into ribbons

Salt and Pepper, to taste

10 fresh Basil leaves, to serve

Directions:

- Heat your grill to medium-low. Place the broccoli, drizzle with the oil and season with salt and pepper; grill the broccoli until lightly charred, about 6-7 minutes. Set aside.

- Preheat the oven to 350 degrees F. Line a baking tray with parchment paper.

- Meanwhile, in a bowl combine the flour, yogurt and salt to form a dough.

- Transfer the dough onto the lined baking tray and shape into a rough circle.

- Spread the tomato puree, dry oregano and top with the Mozzarella.

- Arrange over the zucchini and charred broccoli.

- Bake for 15 minutes or until the pizza is turning firm and golden and the cheese is completely melted.

- Finally, scatter olives and basil leaves and serve immediately.

Crustless Cheeseburger Quiche

Serves: 4 \ Ready in: 40 minutes

Nutritional Info per serving:

Calories 249, Net Carbs 4.1 g, Fat 20.6 g, Protein 10.8 g

Ingredients:

6 large Eggs

¼ cup Spinach, cut into small pieces

½ cup Feta cheese crumbled

½ cup Parmesan cheese, grated

½ cup Mushrooms, sliced

¼ cup Heavy cream

½ Onion, diced

1 tbsp Avocado oil

1 large Zucchini, thinly sliced

2 Tomatoes, thinly sliced

1 dash Coarse salt

Fresh Parsley, to garnish

Directions:

- In a large bowl whisk the eggs. Add the mushrooms, spinach, onion, feta, Parmesan, heavy cream and salt and mix well to combine.

- Preheat your oven to 350 degrees F. Grease a baking dish with avocado oil.

- Pour the mixture into the baking dish, arrange zucchini slices over. Top with tomato slices and bake for 35 minutes, until it is browned around the edges.

- Let it cool for 2 minutes before serving.

- Cut the quiche into 3/4-inch thick slices and serve topped with fresh parsley.

Olive and Basil Turnip Pizza

Serves: 4 \ Ready in: 40 minutes

Nutritional Info per serving:

Calories 168, Net Carbs 3.7 g, Fat 10.1 g, Protein 16.3 g

Ingredients:

1 Turnip, chopped

3 Eggs, beaten

½ cup Marinara sauce

12 large black olives, pitted and sliced

A few Basil leaves, chopped

1 tbsp Olive oil

½ tsp Garlic powder

5 ounces shredded Mozzarella cheese

Directions:

- Preheat your oven to 400 degrees F. Warm the olive oil in a skillet over medium heat. Add the turnip and season with garlic powder.
- Cook until browned, about 10 minutes. Place in a bowl and add the eggs.
- Combine the mixture, mix well and return to the skillet.
- Spread the mixture, covering the bottom of the skillet thoroughly. Bake for 12 minutes.
- Sprinkle the Mozzarella cheese over, and bake for another 5 minutes.
- Place the marinara sauce in a pot and bring to a simmer.
- Pour the sauce over the pizza, and top with basil and olives.

Broccoli Burger with Cucumber

Serves: 2 \ Ready in: 2 hours and 10 minutes

Nutritional Info per serving:

Calories 256, Net Carbs 8.6 g, Fat 11.7 g, Protein 10.7 g

Ingredients:

2 tsp Onion powder

¾ cup Almond flour

½ cup Almond milk

2 2 ½ -inches Broccoli steak slices

½ cup Water

1 tsp Cumin

¼ tsp Salt

1 tsp Paprika

2 tsp Garlic powder

1 tbsp Coconut oil, melted

¼ tsp Black pepper

½ cup Hot sauce

2 romaine Lettuce leaves

2 keto Buns

2 Tomato slices

Slaw:

¼ cup Greek Yogurt

½ English Cucumber, chopped

2 tbsp Vinegar

2 tbsp Dijon mustard

Salt and pepper, to taste

Directions:

- Preheat your oven to 450 degrees F. Line a cooking sheet with waxed paper.

- Whisk together the milk, flour, water, and spices, in a bowl.

- Dredge the broccoli steaks in the mixture, making sure they are well coated. Arrange on the cookie sheet and bake for 25 minutes.

- In a separate bowl combine the coconut oil and hot sauce.

- Coat the broccoli steaks with this mixture, then place them on the baking sheet, insert it in the oven and bake for an additional 25 minutes.

- In a small bowl, whisk together the slaw ingredients and combine them with the chopped cucumber. Cut the keto buns in half.
- Assemble the burgers by placing a steak on one bun half and topping it with the slaw. Top with the other bun half.

Mayo and Broccoli Slaw

Serves: 4 / Preparation Time: 10 minutes

Nutritional Info per serving:

Calories 135, Net Carbs 2.1 g, Fat 10 g, Protein 3 g

Ingredients:

2 tbsp granulated Sugar Substitute

1 tbsp Dijon Mustard

1 tbsp Olive Oil

4 cups Broccoli Slaw

⅓ cup Mayonnaise, sugar-free

1 tsp Celery Seeds

1 ½ tbsp Apple Cider Vinegar

Directions:

- Whisk together all of the ingredients, except for the broccoli, until you obtain a dressing consistency mixture.
- Place the broccoli in a large bowl.
- Pour the dressing over.
- Mix with your hands to combine well.

Philly Cheese Sandwich on Mushrooms

Serves: 6 \ Ready in: 30 minutes

Nutritional Info per serving:

Calories 158, Net Carbs 3.7 g, Fat 14 g, Protein 9 g

Ingredients:

6 Large Portobello Mushroom Caps

2 tbsp Olive oil

1 tsp Oregano

6 slices Provolone cheese

½ tsp Garlic powder

1 Onion, chopped

2 Bell peppers, seeds removed, sliced

Salt and Black pepper, to taste

Directions:

- Preheat your oven to 400 degrees F. Line a cookie sheet with parchment paper.
- Arrange the mushroom caps on the baking dish. Spray with cooking spray. Bake for about 10 minutes.
- Heat the olive oil in a skillet over medium heat. Add the onion and pepper slices. Season with garlic powder, oregano, salt and pepper. Cook for about 10 minutes, or until caramelized.
- Pack each of the portobello caps with the caramelized mixture.
- Top with a slice of provolone cheese. Bake for another 5 minutes and serve immediately.

Tomato and Eggplant Pizza

Serves: 2 \ Ready in: 10 minutes

Nutritional Info per serving:

Calories 377, Net Carbs 5.5 g, Fat 18.8 g, Protein 24.5 g

Ingredients:

1 Eggplant, peeled and sliced	4 Tomato slices
1 tsp Garlic powder	1 tbsp Olive oil
1 tsp Oregano	Salt and Black pepper, to taste
⅓ cup Tomato sauce	Fresh Basil, to garnish
4 fresh Mozzarella slices	Black olives, to garnish
¼ cup Mozzarella cheese, shredded	Cooking spray

Directions:

- Preheat the oven to 400 degrees F. Lightly grease a baking sheet with a nonstick cooking spray.

- Meanwhile, heat the olive oil in a skillet over medium heat. Add the eggplant slices, season with salt, pepper, and garlic powder and cook for about 5 minutes per side.

- Spread the eggplant to cover the bottom of the prepared baking sheet, arrange the Mozzarella slices over and top with the tomato slices.

- Place in the oven and bake for 10 minutes. Spread the tomato sauce over and sprinkle shredded cheese on top.

- Return to the oven and bake for an additional 5 minutes, or until the cheese is melted.

- Serve garnished with fresh basil and black olives.

Chili Green Beans with Zoodles

Serves: 4 \ Ready in: 25 minutes

Nutritional Info per serving:

Calories 104, Net Carbs 2.5 g, Fat 5.5 g, Protein 3.7 g

Ingredients:

½ red Onion, diced

1 tbsp Olive oil

2 Bell peppers, chopped

2 Zucchinis, spiralized

2 Celery stalks, diced

2 Garlic cloves, minced

1 Jalapeno pepper, diced

14 ounces canned Green Beans, drained and rinsed

14 ounces canned diced Tomatoes

1 tbsp Chili powder

2 tbsp Parmesan cheese, freshly grated, to garnish

Salt and Pepper, to taste

Directions:

- Heat the olive oil in a large pot. Add the diced onion, garlic, jalapeno and celery and cook over medium heat until softened, about 5 minutes. Season well. Add the tomatoes, cumin, oregano, chilli powder, bell pepper, and green beans.

- Bring the mixture to a boil, then reduce the heat, and let simmer for 5 minutes. Season with salt and pepper to taste.

- Add the zucchini noodles and let cook, stirring frequently, until the zoodles are just tender, about 4 minutes. Serve topped with Parmesan cheese.

Low-Protein Artichoke Salad

Serves: 4 / Preparation Time: 35 minutes

Nutritional Info per serving:

Calories 213, Net Carbs 6.5 g, Fat 13 g, Protein 8 g

Ingredients:

6 Baby Artichokes

6 cups Water

1 tbsp Lemon Juice

¼ cup Cherry Peppers, halved

¼ cup pitted Olives, sliced

¼ cup Olive Oil

¼ tsp Lemon Zest

2 tsp Balsamic Vinegar, sugar-free

1 tbsp chopped Dill

½ tsp Salt

¼ tsp Black pepper

1 tbsp Capers

Directions:

- Combine the water and salt in a pot over medium heat.
- Trim and halve the artichokes and add to the pot.
- Bring to a boil, then lower the heat, and let simmer for 20 minutes.
- Meanwhile, combine the rest of the ingredients.
- Place the artichokes in a bowl.
- Pour the olive mixture over.
- Toss to combine well and serve as a side dish.

Superfoods Low-Protein Soup

Serves: 6 / Preparation Time: 30 minutes

Nutritional Info per serving:

Calories 177, Net Carbs 2.8 g, Fat 17.6 g, Protein 7.9 g

Ingredients:

1 Cauliflower head, chopped

7 ounces Spinach

1 Onion, chopped

2 Garlic Cloves, minced

5 ounces Watercress

4 cups Veggie Stock

1 cup Coconut Milk

1 tsp Salt

1 tbsp Ghee

1 Bay Leaf

Directions:

1. Melt the ghee in a large pot over medium heat.
2. Stir in the onion and cook for 3 minutes. Add garlic and cook for 1 more minute.
3. Add cauliflower and cook for an additional 5 minutes.
4. Pour the stock over and add the bay leaf.
5. Close the lid, bring to a boil, and then reduce the heat.
6. Simmer for about 3 minutes.
7. Add spinach and watercress, and cook for about 3 more minutes.
8. Stir in the coconut cream and salt.
9. Discard the bay leaf, and blend the soup with a hand blender.

Cold Veggie Soup with Goat Cheese and Avocado

Serves: 6 / Preparation Time: 15 minutes

Nutritional Info per serving:

Calories 627, Net Carbs 8.5 g, Fat 58.8 g, Protein 17.5 g

Ingredients:

2 small Green Peppers, roasted

2 large Red Peppers, roasted

2 Medium Avocados, flesh scoped out

2 Garlic Cloves

2 Spring Onions, chopped

1 Cucumber, chopped

1 cup Olive Oil

2 tbsp Lemon Juice

4 Tomatoes, chopped

7 ounces Goat Cheese

1 small Red Onion, coarsely chopped

2 tbsp Apple Cider Vinegar

Directions:

1. Chop all of the veggies, and scoop out the avocado flesh.
2. Place the peppers, tomatoes, avocado, onion, garlic, lemon juice, olive oil, vinegar, and salt, to a food processor or a blender. Pulse until smooth.
3. Transfer the mixture to a pot. Stir in cucumbers and green onions.
4. Divide between 6 soup bowls. Serve generously topped with goat cheese.

Cheddar and Broccoli Soup

Serves: 4 / Preparation Time: 20 minutes

Nutritional Info per serving:

Calories 515, Net Carbs 3.7 g, Fat 42.3 g, Protein 27.8 g

Ingredients:

¾ cup Heavy cream

1 Onion, diced

1 tsp minced Garlic

4 cups chopped Broccoli

1 ½ cups Veggie broth

3 cups grated Cheddar Cheese

Salt and Pepper, to taste

Directions:

- Combine the broth, broccoli, onion, and garlic, in a large pot. Place over medium heat and bring to a boil. Reduce the heat and simmer for 10 minutes.

- Blend the soup with a hand blender until smooth. Stir in the heavy cream and cook for 3 more minutes. Sprinkle with the cheese and cook until smooth, for about 1 minute.

- Season with salt and pepper, to taste and serve immediately.

Wild Mushroom Soup

Serves: 4 / Preparation Time: 25 minutes

Nutritional Info per serving:

Calories 244, Net Carbs 3.8 g, Fat 15 g, Protein 9.1 g

Ingredients:

¼ cup Butter

5 ounces Crème Fraiche

12 oz fresh Wild Mushrooms, chopped

2 tsp Thyme

2 Garlic Cloves, minced

4 cups Chicken Broth

Directions:

- Melt the butter in a large pot over medium heat. Add garlic and cook for one minute. Add mushrooms, season with salt and pepper, and cook for 7-10 minutes. Pour the broth over and bring to a boil.

- Reduce the heat and simmer for 10 minutes. Blend the mixture with a hand blender until smooth. Stir in crème fraiche.

- Garnish with thyme leaves before serving.

Goat Cheese Bowl with Spinach and Strawberries

Serves: 2 / Preparation Time: 20 minutes

Nutritional Info per serving:

Calories 424, Net Carbs 6.8 g, Fat 34.2 g, Protein 26 g

Ingredients:

2 cups Baby Spinach,

4 Strawberries, sliced

½ cup flaked Almonds

1 ½ cups grated hard Goat Cheese

4 tbsp Raspberry Vinaigrette

Directions:

- Preheat your oven to 400 degrees F.

- Arrange the grated goat cheese in two circles on two pieces of parchment paper. Place in the oven and bake for 10 minutes.

- In two equal bowls, place them upside down, and carefully place the parchment paper on top of them, to give the cheese a bowl-like shape.

- Let cool that way for 15 minutes. Divide the spinach between the bowls.

- Drizzle the vinaigrette over. Serve topped with almond and strawberries.

DINNER

Zucchini Grilled Sandwich

Serves: 4 \ Ready in: 50 minutes

Nutritional Info per serving:

Calories 155, Net Carbs 1.8 g, Fat 10.3 g, Protein 8.8 g

Ingredients:

4 cups Zucchini noodles

2 large Eggs

2 slices Provolone cheese

½ cup Parmesan cheese, shredded

¼ tsp Black pepper

¾ cup Almond flour

Cooking spray

Directions:

- Preheat your oven to 450 degrees F and line a cookie sheet with parchment paper.

- In a separate bowl, beat the eggs, and add flour, black pepper and Parmesan cheese. Stir in the zucchini and mix well to combine.

- Divide the zucchini mixture into 8 patties and place on the cookie sheet. Bake for about 20 minutes, turning over once.

- To make the sandwiches, place one provolone cheese slice between 2 zucchini patties.

- Preheat your grill on high. Grill the cheese sandwiches for 2-3 minutes on each side until the cheese is melted.

Lemony Kohlrabi Salad with Feta

Serves: 2 \ Ready in: 15 minutes plus 30 minutes chilling

Nutritional Info per serving:

Calories 293, Net Carbs 3.7 g, Fat 25 g, Protein 12 g

Ingredients:

1 large kohlrabi, trimmed and thinly sliced

2 large radishes, thinly sliced

3 Asparagus spears, shaved (with a veggie peeler)

1 cup Feta cheese, crumbled

2 tbsp Apple Cider Vinegar

Juice of half Lemon

1 tbsp Olive oil

1 tbsp chives, chopped

1 tbsp Stevia

1 tbsp roasted Sunflower seeds

Salt and Black pepper, to taste

Directions:

- For the dressing, mix the olive oil, lemon, chives, vinegar, stevia, salt and pepper in a large bowl. Whisk to combine.

- Arrange kohlrabi, radishes, and asparagus on a serving plate and pour the dressing over. Toss to coat well.

- Top with Feta cheese and roasted sunflower seeds.

- Let sit for about 30 minutes in the fridge before serving.

Zucchini Vegetable Pie

Serves: 4 \ Ready in: 30 minutes

Nutritional Info per serving:

Calories 568, Net Carbs 6.2 g, Fat 52 g, Protein 21.9 g

Ingredients:

3 Eggs

¾ cup Coconut flour

2 tbsp Sunflower seeds

½ tbsp Sesame seeds

½ cup Butter, melted

A pinch of salt

½ tbsp chia seeds

Filling:

¼ cup Carrots, thinly sliced

1 Zucchini, thinly sliced

8 Eggs

½ tbsp dried Parsley

¾ cup mayonnaise

½ tsp Onion powder

Salt and Black pepper, to taste

Directions:

- To make the dough, combine sunflower and sesame seeds, coconut flour, chia seeds and a pinch of salt, in a food processor and pulse for 1 minute.

- Gradually add eggs and butter while the processor is running; about 30 seconds until evenly combined.

- Take the obtained dough out, form into a flat disk, wrap in clingfilm and refrigerate until ready to use, at least 30 minutes.

- Preheat your oven to 350 degrees F.

- Spread coconut flour on a working surface. Using a rolling pin roll out and away. Repeat until dough is enough to cover the surface of the pie pan.

- Divide the dough evenly into 4 pieces (or more). Bake the crust for 6 minutes. Remove from the oven.
- To make the filling, combine eggs, mayonnaise and spices.
- Arrange the carrot and zucchini slices in the pre-baked pie. Pour the egg mixture over and bake for about 20-25 minutes, until set and golden brown.
- Serve with green salad.

Rich Veggie Wrap

Serves: 4 \ Ready in: 25 minutes

Nutritional Info per serving:

Calories 147, Net Carbs 3.6 g, Fat 10.2 g, Protein 6.1 g

Ingredients:

½ cup full-fat egg Mayonnaise

4 fresh Lettuce leaves

1 small Avocado, Sliced

1 large Carrot, Sliced

1 Beet, diced

1 English Cucumber, sliced

4 pinches of Sprouts

2 cups Spinach

Salt and Pepper, to taste

Directions:

- On a flat surface, lay out one lettuce leaf.
- Spoon ¼ of the mayonnaise, and top with ¼ of each of the remaining ingredients.
- Tuck in the ends of the lettuce and roll each one up, secure it with a toothpick.
- Repeat the process with the rest of the ingredients.

BBQ Zucchini Burgers

Serves: 4 \ Ready in: 1 hour

Nutritional Info per serving:

Calories 238, Net Carbs 7.2 g, Fat 11.5 g, Protein 14.4 g

Ingredients:

4 slices fresh Mozzarella cheese

2 Zucchinis, peeled and shredded

1 red Onion, peeled and sliced

½ tsp Coconut oil

4 keto burger Buns

Salt and Pepper, to taste

BBQ Sauce:

1 tsp salt

1 tbsp Lime juice

3 Garlic cloves

¼ cup Stevia

½ cup Tomato sauce

1 tsp Coconut oil

1 tbsp Cilantro

¼ tsp cayenne pepper

¼ tsp Cumin

¼ tsp white Pepper

1 tbsp Dark Molasses

¼ cup Apple Cider Vinegar

1 Pepper from a can of Peppers in Adobo Sauce, seeded

Directions:

- Preheat the oven to 385 degrees F. Line a baking dish with waxed paper.

- Place the zucchini and onions on the baking dish and drizzle with the coconut oil. Season with salt and pepper. Cover the dish with aluminium foil and bake for 20 minutes. Uncover and bake for an additional 10 minutes, until the vegetables are lightly caramelized.

- Meanwhile, place all of the sauce ingredients in a blender or food processor, and blend until smooth.

- Transfer the sauce to a pan and place over medium heat. Bring to a boil, reduce the heat, and let simmer for 20 minutes.

- Add the roasted vegetables to the sauce and stir to combine thoroughly.

- Divide between the buns, add a slice of the Mozzarella and serve.

Pomodoro Zoodles

Serves: 2 \ Ready in: 25 minutes

Nutritional Info per serving:

Calories 174, Net Carbs 3.3 g, Fat 10.2 g, Protein 8.1 g

Ingredients:

2 ¼ cups spiralized Zucchini

14 ounces Tomatoes, crushed

½ cup Onion, diced

½ tbsp Garlic, minced

1 ½ tbsp Basil, chopped

1 tbsp Olive oil

¼ cup Pecorino Romano cheese, grated

Salt and pepper, to taste

Directions:

- Heat the oil in a skillet and cook the garlic until fragrant, for about a minute.

- Add onions and cook for 2 minutes. Stir in the tomatoes and basil.

- Cook for 6 more minutes, stirring occasionally. Stir in the zoodles and cook for 5 more minutes. Season with salt and pepper, and give it a good stir.

- Serve topped with Pecorino Romano cheese.

Spinach and Mushroom Casserole with Celery Rice

Serves: 6 \ Ready in: 1 hour and 30 minutes

Nutritional Info per serving:

Calories 149, Net Carbs 3.9 g, Fat 9.4 g, Protein 8.5 g

Ingredients:

1 large Celery root, cubed

1 cup Vegetable broth

8 oz baby Portobello Mushrooms, quartered

3 Eggs

2 Garlic cloves, minced

2 tbsp Olive oil

1 Onion, diced

½ tsp Nutmeg

10 ounces Spinach

1.5 cups Coconut milk

Salt and pepper, to taste

Finely chopped Parsley, to garnish

Directions:

- Preheat your oven to 325 degrees F.
- Pulse the celeriac cubes in your food processor until rice is formed. Set aside.
- Heat the oil in a skillet over medium heat and cook the onion for 3 minutes.
- Add garlic and cook for another 1 minute. Stir in mushrooms and cook for an additional 5 minutes.
- Finally, add spinach, and cook for 2 minutes.Taste and adjust the seasonings.
- In a bowl, whisk together the eggs, broth, nutmeg, and milk.
- In a greased baking dish place the celeriac rice in an even layer and veggies on top. Pour the egg mixture over. Bake for about 50 minutes, or until golden.
- Transfer to a serving plate, garnish with parsley and serve immediately.

Spicy Carrot Risotto with Cheddar

Serves: 2 \ Ready in: 25 minutes

Nutritional Info per serving:

Calories 342, Net Carbs 7.3 g, Fat 25.8 g, Protein 10.9 g

Ingredients:

2 large Carrots, cubed

1 Onion, diced

3 tsp diced Jalapeno

Juice of 1 Lime

½ cup Cheddar cheese, grated

1 tbsp Olive oil

½ tsp Chili powder

½ cup Vegetable broth

1 tbsp Cilantro, chopped

½ Avocado, sliced

Salt and pepper, to taste

Directions:

- Pulse the carrot cubes in your food processor until rice is formed. Set aside.
- Heat the olive oil in a skillet over medium heat.
- Cook the onion for about 3 minutes, or until soft.
- Stir in the rice, cilantro, lime juice, broth, jalapenos, and chili powder.
- Season with salt and pepper. Cook for about 10 minutes.
- Serve topped with avocado.

Broccoli Risotto with Green Beans and Peppers

Serves: 2 \ Ready in: 30 minutes

Nutritional Info per serving:

Calories 191, Net Carbs 7.9 g, Fat 10.7 g, Protein 12.6 g

Ingredients:

1 Broccoli, cut into small florets

2 Scallions, diced

2 Eggs, beaten

½ cup Green Beans

1 Garlic clove, minced

1 tsp Olive oil

½ cup diced Bell peppers

1 tsp Tamari sauce

Salt and pepper, to taste

¼ cup grated Parmigiano-Reggiano cheese

Fresh Parsley, to garnish

Directions:

- Place the broccoli florets in the food processor and pulse to form rice. Set aside.

- Heat the oil in a skillet and cook the bell peppers, scallions, and garlic, for about 3 minutes, or until tender. Add the broccoli rice and cook for 2 more minutes.

- Crack the eggs into the skillet, scramble them; add green beans and tamari. Taste and adjust the seasonings. Cook for a couple of minutes, until the green beans are softened.

- Top with Parmesan cheese and serve warm over the broccoli risotto sprinkled with fresh parsley.

Creamy Mushrooms & Rutabaga Rice

Serves: 2 \ Ready in: 20 minutes

Nutritional Info per serving:

Calories 385, Net Carbs 7.7 g, Fat 17.6 g, Protein 15.7 g

Ingredients:

1 Rutabaga, cubed

1 tsp Thyme

4 tbsp Parmesan cheese

4 ounces Button Mushrooms, sliced

⅓ cup yellow Onions, chopped

1 Garlic clove, minced

¼ cup Heavy cream

½ tbsp Coconut oil

¼ cup Water

Directions:

- Pulse the rutabaga cubes in a food processor to reach a rice-like texture.
- Next, melt the coconut oil in a skillet over medium heat.
- Add in onion and garlic and cook them until lightly browned and fragrant, for about 3 minutes.
- Then, add the mushrooms and cook for another 4 minutes.
- Stir in thyme and rutabaga rice and continue cooking for a minute.
- Finally, pour in the water and heavy cream and cook for a further 6 minutes, stirring periodically.
- Serve warm topped with Parmesan cheese.

Two-Cheese Garlic Zoodles

Serves: 2 \ Ready in: 15 minutes

Nutritional Info per serving:

Calories 216, Net Carbs 4.9 g, Fat 16.4 g, Protein 10.5 g

Ingredients:

2 Celery stalks, diced

2 Garlic cloves, minced

4 large Zucchinis, spiralized

2 Tomatoes, cut into 4 pieces each

2 ½ tsp Oregano lakes

1 tbsp Butter

½ cup Vegetable broth

½ red Onion, diced

¼ cup Cheddar cheese, grated

¼ cup Parmesan cheese, grated

Salt and pepper, to taste

Fresh Basil, to garnish

Directions:

- Melt the butter in a skillet over medium heat.

- Add onions and celery and cook for 3 minutes. Add garlic and cook for 30 seconds. Stir in oregano.

- Remove the vegetables to a plate and set aside.

- In the same skillet add the tomatoes and cook, stirring occasionally, until they start to burst, about 4 minutes.

- Pour the broth in the skillet to deglaze the pan, stirring to scrape browned bits from the cooking surface.

- Stir zucchini into the broth and cook, stirring occasionally, until tender-crisp, about 2 minutes.

- Stir in basil through the zoodles.

- Top with Parmesan and Cheddar cheese before serving.

Spiralized Cucumber Salad with Avocado

Serves: 4 \ Ready in: 5 minutes

Nutritional Info per serving:

Calories 213, Net Carbs 3.8 g, Fat 15.8 g, Protein 8.5 g

Ingredients:

1 Avocado, sliced

1 large Cucumber, spiralized

6 cups Romaine salad, chopped

Dressing:

½ cup full-fat Yogurt

1 tbsp Olive oil

1 Garlic clove, pressed

3 tbsp Lemon juice

¼ tsp salt

¼ cup Parmesan cheese, grated

2 tsp Worcestershire sauce

1 tsp Dijon mustard

A pinch of Black pepper

Directions:

- Whisk together all of the dressing ingredients in a jar with a lid. Seal the jar and shake vigorously to emulsify.

- Arrange the romaine lettuce, cucumber, and avocado in a nice serving platter.

- Pour dressing over mixture and serve.

Delicious Tofu Stew

Serves: 4 \ Ready in: 55 minutes

Nutritional Info per serving:

Calories 203, Net Carbs 3.8 g, Fat 14.8 g, Protein 13.5 g

Ingredients:

14 oz firm Tofu, drained and cubed

2 tbsp Olive oil

½ small Cabbage, shredded

1 Onion, chopped

1 Garlic clove, crushed

2 Zucchinis, sliced

1 cup Vegetable broth

14 oz canned Tomatoes, chopped

1 Bay leaf

Sea salt freshly ground pepper, to taste

Directions:

- Heat the oil in a heavy-bottomed pan over moderate heat. Add the garlic and onion and cook until soft, about 3 minutes. Add the tofu and cook for another 4 minutes.
- Stir in all the vegetables, bay leaf, and pour in the vegetable broth. Season to taste with salt and pepper.
- Bring the stew to a boil and let it imbue for 40-50 minutes.
- Remove the bay leaf, then serve.

Squash Spaghetti with Broccoli and Cashews Sauce

Serves: 4 \ Ready in: 35 minutes

Nutritional Info per serving:

Calories 455, Net Carbs 6.8 g, Fat 31.5 g, Protein 14.4 g

Ingredients:

3 cups Broccoli florets

1 Butternut squash, spiralized

1 tbsp Olive oil

1 Garlic clove, minced

½ tsp salt

2 tbsp nutritional Yeast

2 tsp Lemon juice

1 tbsp minced shallots

¾ cup Cashews

½ cup Veggie broth

½ cup grated Parmesan cheese

Salt and pepper, to taste

Directions:

- For the sauce, place the salt, garlic, lemon juice, shallots, cashews, yeast, and veggie broth, in a food processor. Pulse until smooth.

- Season with salt and pepper and set aside.

- Preheat your oven to 400 degrees F.

- Arrange the spaghetti on a lined baking sheet and bake for 12 minutes.

- Meanwhile, heat the oil in a skillet, and cook the broccoli for 4 minutes.

- Add the spaghetti to the skillet, pour the sauce over, and stir to combine.

- Serve topped with Parmesan cheese.

Bell Pepper Eggplant Pasta

Serves: 3 \ Ready in: 40 minutes

Nutritional Info per serving:

Calories 245, Net Carbs 4.9 g, Fat 12.6 g, Protein 7.3 g

Ingredients:

2 tbsp Olive oil

½ tsp dried Oregano

½ cup canned Tomato sauce

2 green Bell peppers, spiralized

½ tsp Cumin

¼ cup quartered Olives

½ cup chopped Onions

1 medium Eggplant, sliced

2 Garlic cloves, minced

¼ cup grated Grana Padano cheese

Salt and pepper, to taste

Directions:

- Sprinkle the eggplant slices with salt and let sit for 20 minutes.
- Heat 1 tablespoon of olive oil in a skillet and cook the pepper noodles until "al dente", for about 5 minutes. Then, transfer to a bowl.
- Add the garlic and onions in the same skillet, and cook for 3 minutes.
- Transfer to another bowl.
- Rinse the eggplant pieces and pat dry with kitchen paper.
- Brush with the remaining oil and place in the hot skillet. Fry for 2 to 3 minutes on each side until golden brown.
- In a serving plate, place the pepper noodles topped with the fried eggplant slices and pour over the sautéed onion and garlic.
- Top with Grana Padano cheese and serve.

Pesto and Kale Beet Pasta

Serves: 3 \ Ready in: 25 minutes

Nutritional Info per serving:

Calories 286, Net Carbs 4.1 g, Fat 25 g, Protein 3 g

Ingredients:

2 Beets, spiralized

2 cups Kale

½ tbsp Olive oil

Pesto:

¼ cup Olive oil

3 cups Basil leaves

½ tsp Sea salt

1 Garlic clove, minced

¼ tsp Black pepper

¼ cup pine Nuts

Directions:

- Preheat the oven to 425 degrees F.
- Arrange the beet noodles on a lined baking dish and drizzle the oil over.
- Bake for 8-10 minutes.
- Place all of the pesto ingredients in a food processor and pulse until smooth.
- Combine the noodles and pesto in a serving bowl. Stir in the kale and serve warm.

Pasta Primavera

Serves: 3 \ Ready in: 35 minutes

Nutritional Info per serving:

Calories 162, Net Carbs 5.8 g, Fat 10.5 g, Protein 8.4 g

Ingredients:

1 ½ cups Broccoli florets

2 medium Zucchini, spiralized

½ cup Green Beans

3 tsp Garlic, minced

1 tbsp Olive oil

¼ tsp Red pepper flakes

1 cup Tomatoes, cubed

1 Bell pepper, sliced

2 tbsp Lemon Juice

2 Carrots, shaved

½ cup Parmesan cheese, grated

2 tbsp Parsley, chopped

½ red Onion, sliced

Salt and pepper, to taste

Directions:

- Bring a pot filled with water to a boil over medium heat. Add the broccoli and cook for 2 minutes. Drain and set aside. Heat the olive oil in a skillet and add the onions, garlic, and red pepper flakes.

- Cook for 3 minutes. Add green beans, bell peppers, tomatoes, and cook for 3 more minutes. Stir in zoodles, carrot, parsley, and lemon juice, and cook for 3 another minutes.

- Stir in broccoli and top with Parmesan cheese.

Cabbage & Tomato Zucchini Spaghetti

Serves: 2 \ Ready in: 20 minutes

Nutritional Info per serving:

Calories 240, Net Carbs 3.2 g, Fat 19.1 g, Protein 12.5 g

Ingredients:

1 ½ Zucchinis, spiralized

¾ can (14-ounce one) Tomatoes, diced

1 tsp Red pepper flakes

1 tbsp Oregano

1 ½ cup Kale, chopped

½ Onion, chopped

1 cup Cabbage, shredded

1 Garlic clove, minced

1 tbsp Olive oil

½ cup Cheddar cheese, grated

Salt and pepper, to taste

Directions:

- Firstly, heat the olive oil in a skillet over medium heat and cook the onions for 3 minutes. Add garlic and red pepper flakes and cook for 30 seconds.

- Add in tomatoes and oregano, and cook for 10 minutes, stirring occasionally. Stir in kale and zoodles and remove from heat. Set aside. Coat another skillet with cooking spray. Cook cabbage over medium heat for about 5 minutes, or until tender.

- In a serving plate arrange zoodle mixture and top with the cabbage.

- Serve sprinkled with Cheddar cheese.

Bell Pepper Omelet with Onions and Tomatoes

Serves: 1 \ Ready in: 15 minutes

Nutritional Info per serving:

Calories 415, Net Carbs 6.1 g, Fat 33.1 g, Protein 15.6 g

Ingredients:

1 tsp Olive oil

1 Bell pepper, chopped

½ small Onion, chopped

⅓ cup diced Tomatoes, diced

¼ Avocado, sliced

¼ tsp dry Thyme

2 large Eggs

Salt and ground Black pepper, to taste

Directions:

- Heat the olive oil in a skillet over medium heat.
- Tip in the onion and bell pepper, and cook for about 5 minutes until the onion is just starting to soften.
- Meanwhile, in a bowl, lightly beat the eggs and stir in the thyme. Season with salt and pepper.
- Pour the beaten eggs over the vegetables and sprinkle the tomatoes on top.
- After 3 minutes, flip the omelet over and cook for an additional 3 minutes.
- Serve the omelet topped with avocado slices.

Mediterranean Salad

Serves: 3 \ Ready in: 10 minutes

Nutritional Info per serving:

Calories 282, Net Carbs 5.2 g, Fat 19.4 g, Protein 16 g

Ingredients:

1 clove Garlic, minced

1 tsp fresh Parsley

1 tbsp Milk

2 tbsp Sour cream

2 tbsp Mayonnaise

3 large hard-boiled Eggs, sliced

4 ounces Manchego cheese, cubed

3 cups Iceberg Lettuce, torn into pieces

2 Tomatoes, sliced

1 Bell pepper, chopped

1 medium-sized Cucumber, sliced

1 tablespoon Dijon mustard

Sea salt, to taste

Directions:

- Start by preparing the dressing by mixing the sour cream, mayonnaise, milk, dill, and mustard.
- Season with salt and pepper to taste and gently stir to combine well.
- Arrange the fresh veggies, cheese, and sliced egg in a nice salad platter, place the dijon mustard in the center.
- Drizzle with the prepared dressing and serve well-chilled.

Cheesy Thyme Gofres

Serves: 3 \ Ready in: 35 minutes

Nutritional Info per serving:

Calories 334, Net Carbs 6.2 g, Fat 25 g, Protein 21 g

Ingredients:

3 cups Cauliflower, riced

¾ cup Colby cheese, finely shredded

¾ cup Kale, chopped

¼ cup Parmesan cheese

2 Eggs

2 stalks green Onion, chopped

1 tbsp Olive oil

2 tbsp fresh Thyme, chopped

1 tbsp Garlic powder

Salt and ground Black pepper, to taste

Cooking spray

Directions:

- Add the cauliflower rice, kale, onions, and thyme in a food processor. Blend until everything is well combined.

- Transfer the mixture to a large mixing bowl, add the rest of the ingredients, and mix together until a loose batter is formed.

- Heat the waffle iron and grease with cooking spray.

- Ladle the batter into the hot waffle iron and cook until golden and crisp, about 5 minutes.

- Once cooked, remove from waffle iron and serve hot.

Three Cheese Stuffed Peppers

Serves: 4 \ Ready in: 35 minutes

Nutritional Info per serving:

Calories 243, Net Carbs 5.6 g, Fat 15 g, Protein 12 g

Ingredients:

4 medium green Bell peppers, seeded and halved lengthwise

4 large Eggs

½ cup Cottage cheese

½ cup Queso fresco

½ cup grated Grana Padano

2 cloves Garlic

½ Tomato pulp

¼ tsp fresh Cilantro leaves, chopped

¼ cup Swiss Chard, chopped

Cooking spray

Directions:

- Heat your oven to 350 degrees F. Lightly grease a baking dish with cooking spray.

- In a food processor, blend the cottage cheese, queso fresco, eggs, garlic, swiss chard, tomato pulp, and coriander.

- Fill the bell peppers with the egg mixture and transfer the peppers to the prepared baking dish.

- Cover with foil and bake for 30-40 minutes.

- Remove the foil, sprinkle with Grana Padano cheese and cook for another 5 minutes or until the tops are golden.

Eggs in Parsnip Nests

Serves: 2 \ Ready in: 15 minutes

Nutritional Info per serving:

Calories 175, Net Carbs 2.8 g, Fat 15.1 g, Protein 6.1 g

Ingredients:

½ parsnip, shredded

1 tsp Garlic powder

2 Eggs

1 ½ tbsp Butter

¼ cup baby Arugula

Hot sauce, to garnish

Salt and pepper, to taste

Directions:

- Melt ½ tablespoon of the butter in a skillet over medium heat. Add the parsnip, garlic powder and cook for 10 minutes. Transfer to a bowl.

- Melt half of the remaining butter in the same skillet. Add half of the cooked parsnip and make a hole in the middle.

- Crack an egg in the hole and cook until the egg is set. Repeat the process one more time. Serve topped with arugula and hot sauce.

Fried Faux Mac and Cheese

Serves: 7 / Preparation Time: 45 minutes

Nutritional Info per serving:

Calories 175, Net Carbs 2 g, Fat 12.8 g, Protein 12.6 g

Ingredients:

1 Cauliflower Head, riced

1 ½ cups shredded Cheese

2 tsp Paprika

¾ tsp Rosemary

2 tsp Turmeric

3 Eggs

Oil, for frying

Directions:

1. Microwave the cauliflower for 5 minutes. Place it in cheesecloth and squeeze the extra juices out.
2. Then, transfer the cauliflower to a bowl. Stir in the rest of the ingredients.
3. Heat the oil in a deep pan until it reaches 360 degrees F.
4. Add the above-prepared mixture and fry until golden and crispy.
5. Drain on paper towels before serving.

Buffalo Cheese Salad with Tomatoes

Serves: 4 \ Ready in: 10 minutes

Nutritional Info per serving:

Calories 213, Net Carbs 2.1 g, Fat 13 g, Protein 16 g

Ingredients:

4 Tomatoes, sliced

1 cup fresh Basil leaves, chopped

2 large balls fresh Buffalo cheese, drained and sliced

1 tbsp Capers, drained

2 tbsp Extra-Virgin Olive oil

2 ounces Black Olives, to garnish

Sea salt, to taste

Directions:

- Arrange the salad on a serving platter with two slices of tomato for every piece of cheese. Season to taste with salt.
- Top with the basil leaves and drizzle with olive oil.
- Scatter the black olive and capers over the salad before serving.

Cheesy Bell Pepper Pizza

Serves: 2 / Preparation Time: 40 minutes

Nutritional Info per serving:

Calories 313, Net Carbs 6.7 g, Fat 13.9 g, Protein 38.1 g

Ingredients:

6 ounces Mozzarella

2 tbsp Cream Cheese

2 tbsp Parmesan Cheese

1 tsp Oregano

½ cup Almond Flour

2 tbsp Psyllium Husk

Toppings:

4 ounces grated Cheddar Cheese

¼ cup Marinara Sauce

1 Bell Pepper, sliced

1 Tomato, sliced

2 tbsp chopped Basil

Directions:

1. Preheat the oven to 400 degrees F.
2. Combine all of the crust ingredients in a large bowl, except the Mozzarella.
3. Melt the Mozzarella in a microwave. Stir it into the bowl. Mix with your hands to combine. Divide the obtained dough in two.
4. Roll out the two crusts in circles and place on a lined baking sheet. Bake for about 10 minutes. Scatter the toppings.
5. Return to the oven and bake for another 10 minutes.

Mediterranean Pasta

Serves: 4 / Preparation Time: 15 minutes

Nutritional Info per serving:

Calories 175, Net Carbs 4.2 g, Fat 18.3 g, Protein 6.5 g

Ingredients:

¼ cup sun-dried Tomatoes

5 Garlic Cloves, minced

2 tbsp Butter

1 cup Spinach

2 Large Zucchinis, spiralized (or peeled with a veggie peeler if you don't have a spiralizer)

¼ cup crumbled Feta cheese

¼ cup Parmesan cheese

10 Kalamata Olives, halved

2 tbsp Olive Oil

2 tbsp chopped Parsley

Directions:

1. Heat the olive oil in a pan over medium heat.

2. Add zoodles, butter, garlic, and spinach. Cook for about 5 minutes.

3. Stir in the olives, tomatoes, and parsley. Cook for 2 more minutes.

4. Mix in the Feta cheese and serve sprinkled with Parmesan cheese.

Fake Mushroom Risotto

Serves: 4 / Preparation Time: 15 minutes

Nutritional Info per serving:

Calories 330, Net Carbs 8.4 g, Fat 21.8 g, Protein 15.1 g

Ingredients:

2 Shallots, diced

3 tbsp Olive Oil

¼ cup Veggie broth

⅓ cup Parmesan Cheese

4 tbsp Butter

3 tbsp chopped Chives

2 pounds Mushrooms, sliced

4 ½ cups riced Cauliflower

Directions:

- Heat 2 tbsp of oil in a saucepan. Add the mushrooms and cook over medium heat for about 3 minutes. Remove from pan and set aside.

- Heat the remaining oil and cook the shallots for 2 minutes.

- Stir in the cauliflower and broth, and cook until the liquid is absorbed.

- Add in the rest of the ingredient and stir. Serve warm.

Stuffed Portobellos with Blue Cheese

Serves: 2 / Preparation Time: 30 minutes

Nutritional Info per serving:

Calories 374, Net Carbs 2.5 g, Fat 29 g, Protein 17.4 g

Ingredients:

4 Portobello Mushrooms

2 tbsp Olive Oil

2 cups Lettuce

1 cup crumbled Blue Cheese

Directions:

- Preheat your oven to 350 degrees F. Remove the stems from the mushrooms.
- Fill the mushrooms with blue cheese and place on a lined baking sheet. Bake for about 20 minutes.
- Serve with drizzled with olive oil lettuce.

Vegetarian Ketogenic Burgers

Serves: 2 / Preparation Time: 20 minutes

Nutritional Info per serving:

Calories 415, Net Carbs 2.5 g, Fat 35 g, Protein 19.3 g

Ingredients:

1 Garlic Cloves, minced

2 Portobello Mushrooms

1 tbsp Coconut Oil, melted

1 tbsp chopped Basil

1 tbsp Oregano

2 Eggs, fried

2 Keto Buns

2 tbsp Mayonnaise

2 Lettuce Leaves

Directions:

- Combine the melted coconut oil, garlic, herbs, and salt, in a bowl. Place the mushrooms in the bowl and coat well. Preheat the grill to medium.
- Slice the mushrooms and grill them about 2 minutes per side.
- Cut the keto buns in half. Add the lettuce leaves, then the grilled mushrooms, then the eggs, and finally the mayonnaise. Top with the other bun half.

Thyme and Collard Green Waffles

Serves: 4 / Preparation Time: 45 minutes

Nutritional Info per serving:

Calories 198, Net Carbs 3.5 g, Fat 13.3 g, Protein 16 g

Ingredients:

2 Green Onions, stalks

1 tbsp Olive Oil

2 Eggs

⅓ cup Parmesan Cheese

1 cup Collard Greens

1 cup Mozzarella Cheese

½ Cauliflower Head, chopped

1 tsp Garlic Powder

1 tbsp Sesame Seeds

2 tsp chopped Thyme

Directions:

- Place cauliflower in the food processor and process until rice is formed.
- Add collard greens, spring onions, and thyme to the food processor. Pulse until smooth.
- Transfer to a bowl.
- Stir in the rest of the ingredients and mix to combine.
- Heat your waffle iron and spread the mixture evenly onto the iron.
- Cook for 3-4 minutes and serve immediately.

White Egg Tex Mex Pizza

Serves: 1 / Preparation Time: 17 minutes

Nutritional Info per serving:

Calories 591, Net Carbs 2 g, Fat 49 g, Protein 19 g

Ingredients:

2 Eggs

1 tbsp Water

½ Jalapeno, diced

1 ounce Monterey Jack, shredded

1 tbsp chopped Green Onion

⅛ cup Egg Alfredo Sauce

¼ tsp Cumin

2 tbsp Olive Oil

Directions:

- Preheat the oven to 350 degrees F.
- Heat the olive oil in a skillet over medium heat.
- Whisk the eggs along with water and cumin in a skillet.
- Pour the eggs into the skillet. Cook until set.
- Top with the alfredo sauce and the diced jalapeno pepper.
- Sprinkle the green onions and cheese over.
- Place the skillet in the oven and bake at 350 degrees F for 5 minutes.
- Serve and enjoy.

Primavera Spaghetti Squash

Serves: 4 / Preparation Time: 15 minutes

Nutritional Info per serving:

Calories 223, Net Carbs 5.8 g, Fat 18.2 g, Protein 6.9 g

Ingredients:

1 tbsp Butter

1 cup Cherry Tomatoes

2 tbsp Parsley

4 Bacon Slices

¼ cup Parmesan Cheese

3 tbsp Scallions, chopped

1 cup Sugar Snap Peas

1 tsp Lemon Zest

2 cups cooked Spaghetti Squash

Directions:

- Melt the butter in a saucepan and cook the bacon until crispy.
- Add the tomatoes and peas, and cook for 5 more minutes.
- Stir in parsley, zest, and scallions, and remove the pan from the heat.
- Stir in spaghetti squash and sprinkle with Parmesan cheese to serve.

Vegan Olive and Avocado Zoodles

Serves: 4 / Preparation Time: 15 minutes

Nutritional Info per serving:

Calories 449, Net Carbs 6.4 g, Fat 42 g, Protein 6.3 g

Ingredients:

4 Zucchinis, julienned or spiralized

½ cup Paleo Pesto

2 Avocados, sliced

1 cup Kalamata Olives, chopped

¼ cup chopped Basil

2 tbsp Olive Oil

¼ cup chopped Sun-Dried Tomatoes

Directions:

* Heat half of the olive oil in a pan over medium heat. Add zoodles and cook for 4 minutes. Transfer to a serving bowl.

* Stir in olive oil, pesto, basil, salt, tomatoes, and olives. Top with avocado slices.

SNACKS AND SIDE DISHES

Garlicky Green Beans and Gruyere Casserole

Serves: 4 \ Ready in: 1 hour and 15 minutes

Nutritional Info per serving:

Calories 203, Net Carbs 6.45 g, Fat 12.1 g, Protein 9.2 g

Ingredients:

1 tbsp Coconut oil

1 ½ tbsp fresh Thyme leaves

3 pounds Green Beans

3 Garlic cloves, minced

3 tbsp Parmesan cheese, grated

1 ½ tbsp Gruyere cheese, finely grated

1 Onion, chopped

½ cup Vegetable broth

Cooking spray

Directions:

- Melt the coconut oil in a saucepan over medium heat, and cook the onion for about 3 minutes. Add garlic and cook for another minute.

- Pour the broth, season with salt and pepper, and let simmer for 5 minutes.

- Preheat your oven to 400 degrees F.

- Spray a baking dish with cooking spray, and arrange half of the green beans, making an even layer.

- Add half of the onion mixture over, and top with half of the gruyere cheese.

- Repeat the process one more time, and top with Parmesan cheese.

- Cover the dish with aluminium foil and cook for 60 minutes until golden.

- Transfer the mixture to a bowl, and let cool for about 5 minutes, until safe to handle. When cooled, add in the eggs and mix to combine. Divide between the muffin cups. Bake for 15 minutes.

- Serve the cups topped with the Parmesan cheese.

Cheesy Mushrooms Cups

Serves: 4 \ Ready in: 45 minutes

Nutritional Info per serving:

Calories 253, Net Carbs 5.8 g, Fat 15.9 g, Protein 13.7 g

Ingredients:

1 tbsp Olive oil

1 Onion, diced

1 medium Carrot, grated

1 small parsnip, trimmed and grated

1 cup Portobello Mushrooms, chopped

2 Eggs, beaten

1 cup Parmesan cheese, finely grated

¾ cup Tomatoes, chopped

½ tsp Garlic powder

Salt and pepper, to taste

Cooking spray

Directions:

- Preheat your oven to 425 degrees F. Spray a muffin tin with cooking spray.

- Heat the olive oil in a skillet over medium heat. Add the onion, carrots, mushrooms, tomatoes, and parsnip.

- Season with salt, pepper, and add the garlic powder. Cook for 8 minutes, or until the vegetables are tender.

Roasted Spicy Turnips

Serves: 3 \ Ready in: 40 minutes

Nutritional Info per serving:

Calories 155, Net Carbs 4.9 g, Fat 9.1 g, Protein 9.2 g

Ingredients:

3 large Turnips, sliced

1 tsp Paprika

1 tsp Chili powder

1 tsp Garlic powder

1 ½ tbsp Olive oil

Salt and pepper, to taste

Directions:

- Preheat your oven to 425 degrees F. Line a baking sheet with nonstick cooking spray. Place the turnip slices in a bowl, add the spices and drizzle the oil over.

- Mix with your hands until well-coated. Arrange on the prepared baking sheet, and roast for 25 minutes until crispy. Taste, adjust the seasoning and serve warm.

Stir-Fried Kale with Cheddar Cheese

Serves: 2 \ Ready in: 30 minutes

Nutritional Info per serving:

Calories 163, Net Carbs 2.6 g, Fat 14.7 g, Protein 8.4 g

Ingredients:

2 cups Kale, packed

2 Garlic cloves, sliced

½ red chilli, deseeded and sliced

1 tbsp Cheddar cheese, grated

1 tbsp Coconut oil

1 tbsp Soy sauce

Salt and Pepper, to taste

Directions:

- Heat a large frying pan over medium heat and add the coconut oil.
- When the oil is warm, add the garlic and cook until fragrant, for about 2-3 minutes, then add the kale, chilli and soy sauce.
- Cook for another 2 to 3 minutes until tender. Season with salt and pepper.
- Serve with sprinkled Cheddar cheese.

Easy Creamed Spinach

Serves: 2 \ Ready in: 30 minutes

Nutritional Info per serving:

Calories 340, Net Carbs 3.8 g, Fat 26 g, Protein 4.9 g

Ingredients:

1 tbsp Butter

2 tbsp pine Nuts, lightly toasted

1 cup Spinach, roughly chopped

1 medium Onion, finely chopped

1 clove Garlic, minced

1 cup Heavy Cream

½ tsp dried Oregano

Salt and freshly grounded Black pepper, to taste

1 tbsp grated Parmesan cheese, to serve

Directions:

- Melt the butter in a large frying pan over medium heat and add the onion and garlic. Cook for 2 minutes, stirring periodically, until they are softened.
- Add the spinach and cook for another 2-3 minutes.
- Pour in the cream whisking constantly until the white sauce thickens, about 3 minutes. Season to taste with salt and pepper.
- Serve with sprinkled Parmesan cheese.

Broccoli and Cheese Balls

Serves: 4 \ Ready in: 30 minutes

Nutritional Info per serving:

Calories 215, Net Carbs 1.6 g, Fat 17.5 g, Protein 10.4 g

Ingredients for the Balls:

½ cup Broccoli, riced

½ cup Provolone cheese, shredded

¾ cup Almond flour

2 tbsp Olive oil

2 tbsp flaxseed meal

2 Eggs, beaten

Salt and pepper to taste

For The Dip:

¼ cup mayonnaise

¼ cup fresh chopped Dill

Lemon juice from ½ lemon

Salt and Pepper, to taste

Directions:

- To prepare the dip, combine the mayonnaise, lemon juice and dill, in a bowl. Season to taste with salt and pepper, and set aside.
- In another large bowl, mix the cheese, broccoli rice, almond flour, and eggs until everything is well incorporated.
- Shape the batter into balls and coat with the flaxseed meal.
- Heat the oil in a large skillet over medium-high heat.
- Add the balls and fry them on all sides until golden brown, about 5-6 minutes.
- Once ready, transfer to paper towels to soak up excess fat and season to taste.
- Serve the balls with the dip on the side.

Crispy Fennel Salad with Gorgonzola Cheese

Serves: 4 \ Ready in: 30 minutes

Nutritional Info per serving:

Calories 198, Net Carbs 2.6 g, Fat 17 g, Protein 7 g

Ingredients:

3 cups arugula, packed

1 fennel bulb, very finely sliced

2 oz. Gorgonzola cheese, crumbled

2 tsp Pumpkin seeds

2 tbsp Olive oil

½ tsp Dijon mustard

1 tsp Stevia

1 tbsp Sunflower Seeds

1 tsp lemon juice

1 tbsp red Wine Vinegar

¼ cup raw Walnuts, crushed

Sea salt and Pepper, to taste

Directions:

- To make the dressing, whisk together the stevia, lemon juice, olive oil, vinegar, and mustard in a small bowl. Season to taste with salt and pepper.

- Arrange the arugula and fennel slices on a serving plate.

- Top with gorgonzola cheese, then scatter over the pumpkin and sunflower seeds.

- Refrigerate for 10 minutes before serving. Pour the dressing and walnuts over and serve.

Turmeric Veggie Fritters with Avocado salsa

Serves: 5 \ Ready in: 17 minutes

Nutritional Info per serving:

Calories 225, Net Carbs 5.2 g, Fat 15.7 g, Protein 7.5 g

Ingredients:

1 large Zucchini, spiralized

1 large Carrot, spiralized

¾ cup Almond flour

2 Eggs, beaten

2 tbsp Olive oil

1 tsp Turmeric

5 scallions, chopped

1 cup full-fat Sour Cream

1 large Avocado, diced

Juice of ½ Lime

1 red chilli, deseeded and chopped

2 Tomatoes, chopped

1 tbsp fresh Cilantro, roughly chopped

Salt and pepper, to taste

Directions:

- To make the avocado salsa, mash the avocado with a fork in a small bowl, add the red chilli, fresh cilantro, lime juice, and tomatoes.

- Season with salt and mix well; then reserve in the fridge.

- In a large bowl, place the zucchini, flour, eggs, carrots, scallions, and turmeric.

- Mix with your hands until fully combined.

- Make 5 patties out of the mixture.

- Heat the olive oil in a large skillet over medium heat.

- Fry the patties for about 2-3 minutes per side.

- Serve with avocado salsa and sour cream dolloped on top.

Crispy Tofu Sticks

Serves: 4 \ Ready in: 20 minutes

Nutritional Info per serving:

Calories 252, Net Carbs 3.1 g, Fat 22.7 g, Protein 10.8 g

Ingredients:

14-oz package extra-firm Tofu, drained and cut into ¼-inch planks

3 tbsp Olive oil

½ cup Coconut flour

¼ cup Hot sauce

1 tsp Onion powder

1 tsp Garlic powder

½ tsp salt

2 tbsp Coconut oil, melted

1 tbsp White wine vinegar

1 tsp sugar-free Soy sauce

½ cup vegan Ranch dressing

Directions:

- Pat dry tofu planks dry with paper towel.

- Stir coconut flour, onion powder, garlic powder, and salt together in a large bowl. Add in the tofu and toss to coat.

- Heat the olive oil in a nonstick skillet over medium heat. Add a few tofu pieces and cook until golden brown on the bottom, about 5 minutes.

- Flip the pieces and continue cooking until crispy and golden, for about 5 more minutes.

- Remove tofu to a plate lined with a paper towel to soak the excess fat. Repeat the frying process with the remaining tofu pieces, using more oil as needed.

- Now, mix hot sauce, coconut oil, vinegar, and soy sauce together in a large bowl until smooth and fully emulsified. Then, add the tofu and toss to coat.

- Serve tofu sticks with the ranch dressing.

Vegetable Crisps with Homemade Guacamole

Serves: 4 \ Ready in: 35 minutes

Nutritional Info per serving:

Calories 221, Net Carbs 3.5 g, Fat 13.7 g, Protein 4.8 g

Ingredients:

2 Eggplants, finely sliced

1 Turnip, finely sliced

1 Parsnip, finely sliced

1 tbsp Avocado oil, plus extra for greasing

For guacamole:

¼ cup Arugula

1 Avocado, seeded, peeled and chopped

1 green Onion, roughly chopped

1 cup Tomatoes, chopped

2 cloves Garlic, crushed

Juice from 1 Lime

2 tablespoons Cilantro, chopped

Salt, to taste

Directions:

- Preheat your oven to 350 degrees F and grease a large baking tray with a little bit of oil.

- Into a bowl add the eggplant, turnip, and parsnip slices and toss to combine with the avocado oil.

- Transfer the vegetables to the oiled tray and bake for 12 minutes. Flip the vegetables and bake for 8 minutes, until crisp. Let cool on a wire rack.

- Meanwhile, make your guacamole by mixing the avocado, tomato, arugula, green onion, cilantro, garlic, and lemon juice, in a food processor.

- Blend until smooth and season to taste with salt.

- Transfer to a serving bowl and serve with the vegetable crisps.

Baked Eggplant Fries with Cheese and Garlic

Serves: 4 \ Ready in: 35 minutes

Nutritional Info per serving:

Calories 167, Net Carbs 6.5 g, Fat 10.5 g, Protein 5.4 g

Ingredients:

2 Medium Eggplants, sliced into thin rounds

⅓ cup grated Asiago Cheese

2 tbsp Olive Oil

Juice of ¼ lemon

1 clove Garlic, pressed

Cooking spray

Salt and Freshly ground Black pepper to taste

Directions:

- Preheat your oven to 450 degrees F.
- Grease a baking dish with cooking spray.
- Arrange the eggplant slices onto the dish in a single layer.
- Drizzle with olive oil on each side of the slices.
- Season with salt and pepper.
- Bake for about 15 minutes, flipping once until golden brown and crispy.
- Meanwhile, prepare the cheese dip by mixing the cheese, remaining olive oil, lemon juice, and garlic in a small bowl.
- Serve eggplant fries warm or cool with the cheese dip.

Simple Pesto and Asparagus Zoodles

Serves: 2 \ Ready in: 17 minutes

Nutritional Info per serving:

Calories 422, Net Carbs 5.3 g, Fat 37 g, Protein 8.6 g

Ingredients:

1 tsp Olive Oil

4 thick Asparagus Spears, sliced

2 Zucchinis, spiralized

Salt and Pepper, to taste

For the Pesto:

½ cup Parmesan cheese, grated

1 Garlic clove, pressed

¼ cup Olive oil

1 cup Basil

1 tbsp Pine Nuts

Directions:

- Start by preparing the pesto. Mix the basil, Parmesan cheese, pine nuts, and garlic in a food processor.

- While the blender is running, drizzle in olive oil until desired consistency. Season with salt and pepper and keep in the fridge.

- Warm the oil in a skillet over medium heat, add asparagus, and season with salt and pepper. Cook for 5 minutes.

- Add zucchini and cook for 2 more minutes.

- Stir in the pesto sauce and serve.

Spinach Cheesy Puff Balls

Serves: 20 / Preparation Time: 30 minutes

Nutritional Info per serving:

Calories 60, Net Carbs 0.8 g, Fat 5 g, Protein 2 g

Ingredients:

⅓ cup crumbled Feta cheese

¼ tsp Nutmeg

¼ tsp Pepper

3 tbsp Heavy cream

1 tsp Garlic Powder

1 tbsp Onion Powder

4 tbsp Butter, melted

⅓ cup Parmesan Cheese

2 Eggs

16 ounces Spinach

1 cup Almond Flour

Directions:

- Place all of the ingredients in a food processor. Process until smooth.
- Transfer to the freezer for about 10 minutes.
- Remove from the freezer and make balls out of the mixture.
- Arrange them on a lined baking sheet.
- Bake at 350 degrees F for about 10-12 minutes.
- Serve with yogurt if desired.

Fried Artichoke Hearts with Aioli Sauce

Serves: 2 / Preparation Time: 20 minutes

Nutritional Info per serving:

Calories 235, Net Carbs 4.9 g, Fat 21.4 g, Protein 21.2 g

Ingredients:

12 Fresh Baby Artichokes

2 tbsp Lemon Juice

¼ cup Olive oil

Sea Salt, flakes

For Aioli Sauce mix the following:

½ cup Mayonnaise

1 Garlic clove, pressed

Directions:

- Slice the artichokes vertically into narrow wedges. Drain them on paper towels before frying.
- Heat the oil until it reaches 360 degrees F. Fry the artichokes until browned and crispy. Drain on paper towels. Sprinkle with sea salt and lemon juice.
- Serve with a dip of Aioli sauce.

Buttered Asparagus and Green Beans

Serves: 2 \ Ready in: 16 minutes

Nutritional Info per serving:

Calories 136, Net Carbs 3.3 g, Fat 9.7 g, Protein 3.8 g

Ingredients:

2 tbsp Butter

1 cup Green Beans, trimmed

1 cup Asparagus, trimmed

1 tbsp flaked Almonds

Salt and pepper, to taste

Directions:

- Heat a frying pan over medium heat, add the almonds flakes and toast until golden, about 3 to 4 minutes. Transfer to a plate and set aside.

- Cook the asparagus and green beans in a pot of boiling salted water over medium heat for 2 minutes, until tender, then remove to a bowl of ice-cold water, to cool.

- Drain the greens and transfer to the frying pan. Add the butter and fry gently for 1–2 minutes. Season with salt and pepper. Transfer to a platter and sprinkle with the toasted almond flakes.

Parsnip Gratin with Kale

Serves: 4 \ Ready in: 20 minutes

Nutritional Info per serving:

Calories 488, Net Carbs 7.1g, Fat 30 g, Protein 29 g

Ingredients:

2 large Parsnips, grated

2 Garlic cloves, pressed

1 tbsp Olive Oil

3 cups Gouda cheese, shredded

2 ½ tsp Thyme

¼ tsp Red Pepper Flakes

6 cups Kale, packed

Cooking spray

Salt and pepper, to taste

Directions:

- Preheat your oven to 425 degrees F. Spray a baking dish with cooking spray.

- Heat the olive oil in a skillet and add garlic, thyme, and red pepper flakes.

- Cook for 30 seconds, or until softened. Add the kale and cook for a further 4 minutes. Arrange a single layer with ⅓ of the parsnips, top with ⅓ of the kale, and sprinkle 1 cup of Gouda cheese. Repeat the process two more times.

- Cover the dish with foil and bake for 10 minutes, then remove the foil. Cook for another 10 minutes, until golden.

Baked Rutabaga Chips with Yogurt Dip

Serves: 2 \ Ready in: 45 minutes

Nutritional Info per serving:

Calories 218, Net Carbs 6.7 g, Fat 7.9 g, Protein 12.6 g

Ingredients:

1 medium Rutabaga, spiralized with the straight blade

1 tsp Garlic powder

1 tbsp Olive oil

½ cup Greek yogurt, full fat

½ clove Garlic, pressed

1 tbsp fresh Dill, finely chopped

Salt and Pepper, to taste

Directions:

- To make the dip, combine yogurt, garlic, fresh dill, and salt in a small bowl. Mix well and reserve in the fridge.

- Preheat your oven to 375 degrees F. Line a baking sheet with parchment paper.

- Place the rutabaga, olive oil, and garlic powder in a bowl and toss to combine. Season to taste. Arrange the rutabaga on the baking sheet.

- Bake for 35 minutes, turning over halfway through. Serve with the yogurt dip.

Keto Deviled Eggs

Serves: 6 / Preparation Time: 30 minutes

Nutritional Info per serving:

Calories 71, Net Carbs 0.5 g, Fat 5.7 g, Protein 6.1 g

Ingredients:

6 Eggs

1 tbsp Green Tabasco

⅓ cup Sugar-Free Mayonnaise

Directions:

1. Place the eggs in a saucepan and cover with water. Bring to a boil over medium heat. Boil for 8 minutes. Place the eggs in an ice bath and let cool for 10 minutes.
2. Peel and slice them in half. Whisk together the tabasco, mayonnaise, and salt, in a small bowl.
3. Spoon this mixture on top of each egg half and serve immediately.

Basic Cauliflower Fritters

Serves: 12 / Preparation Time: 35 minutes

Nutritional Info per serving:

Calories 69, Net Carbs 2,3 g, Fat 4.5 g, Protein 4.5 g

Ingredients:

1 pound grated Cauliflower

½ cup Parmesan Cheese

3 ounces finely chopped Onion

½ tsp Baking Powder

½ cup Almond Flour

3 Eggs

1 ½ tsp Lemon Pepper

Olive Oil, for frying

Directions:

- Sprinkle the salt over the cauliflower in a bowl, and let it stand for 10 minutes.
- Add in the other ingredients in the bowl. Mix with your hands to combine. Place a skillet over medium heat, and heat some olive oil in it.
- Meanwhile, shape fritters out of the cauliflower mixture. Fry in batches, for about 3 minutes per side.

SWEETS

Flourless Eggplant Muffins with Chocolate

Serves: 12 \ Ready in: 45 minutes

Nutritional Info per serving:

Calories 55, Net Carbs 1.4 g, Fat 2.5 g, Protein 2.4 g

Ingredients:

½ cup Almond Flour

4 large Eggs

2 ounces cocoa powder

¾ tsp Baking Soda

2 tsp Cinnamon

½ tsp Nutmeg

3 tbsp Almond Milk

1 tbsp Cacao Powder

¼ cup xylitol

1 tbsp Butter

1 tbsp pure Vanilla Extract

Directions:

- Preheat your oven to 350 degrees F. Grease 12 muffin cups with cooking spray.
- Combine the dry ingredients in one bowl and whisk the wet ones in another.
- Gently mix in the two mixtures. Stir in cocoa powder.
- Pour the batter into the muffin cups. Bake for 30 minutes.
- Allow your muffins to cool completely before serving.

Chocolate Glazed Avocado Donuts

Serves: 12 \ Ready in: 30 minutes

Nutritional Info per serving:

Calories 121, Net Carbs 2.5 g, Fat 8.7 g, Protein 3.6 g

Ingredients:

1 cup Coconut Flour

3 Eggs

2 tbsp shredded Coconut

3 ounces dark chocolate

3 tbsp Stevia

1 Peach, mashed

1 Avocado, mashed

2 tsp Vanilla Extract

2 tsp Cinnamon

2 tbsp Milk

¼ tsp Salt

1 tbsp Coconut Oil

½ tsp Nutmeg

Directions:

*   Preheat your oven to 350 degrees F, and butter a donut pan.
*   Combine the dry ingredients in one bowl, and whisk the wet ones in another.
*   Combine the two mixtures gently. Stir in the avocado.
*   Pour the batter into the donut pan. Bake for 25-30 minutes.
*   Melt the chocolate chips in a microwave for 1 minute.
*   Spread the chocolate onto the cakes. Let cool completely before serving.

Chocolate and Avocado Truffles

Serves: 12 \ Ready in: 1 hour and 20 minutes

Nutritional Info per serving:

Calories 105, Net Carbs 5.4 g, Fat 8.7 g, Protein 2.9 g

Ingredients:

1 ½ cup dark chocolate

1 Avocado

1 tsp. Vanilla paste

A pinch of Salt

A pinch grated Nutmeg

⅓ cup Cocoa powder for rolling

Directions:

- Firstly, mash the avocado using a fork, in a small bowl.
- Place the chocolate, vanilla paste and pinch of salt in a microwave-safe bowl and melt for 1 minute on medium-high until completely smooth in the microwave.
- Stir in the mashed avocado and combine well until smooth and thickened. Let cool in the fridge for one hour. Once the chocolate mixture is cooled, shape into 12 balls. Place the cocoa powder in a plate, and roll each truffle into the cocoa to coat.

Vanilla Chia Pudding

Serves: 2 \ Ready in: 10 minutes + chilling time: 1 hour

Nutritional Info per serving:

Calories 154, Net Carbs 5.4 g, Fat 8.3 g, Protein 6.2 g

Ingredients:

2 tbsp Chia seeds

1 cup unsweetened Almond milk

1 tbsp pure Vanilla extract

¼ cup Xylitol

1 ½ tbsp Salt

Directions:

- Mix in the chia seeds, almond milk, vanilla extract, xylitol, and salt, in a mixing bowl.

- Refrigerate for 1 hour until the mixture thickens. Add more almond milk as needed, if too thick.

Chocolate Avocado Mousse

Serves: 2 \ Ready in: 10 minutes + chilling time: 1 hour

Nutritional Info per serving:

Calories 441, Net Carbs 6.4 g, Fat 29.3 g, Protein 9.2 g

Ingredients:

1 cup unsweetened Almond milk

1 Avocado, sliced

¼ cup Cacao powder

1 tbsp pure Vanilla extract

½ cup Heavy Cream

2 packets Stevia

6 fresh Strawberries, sliced

¼ cup unsweetened Coconut flakes

Fresh Mint leaves, to garnish

Directions:

- Pour the heavy cream and add the stevia into a deep bowl. Blend with an electric mixer, until fluffy.

- Add in the almond milk, avocado, cacao powder, and vanilla extract and blend again until well combined.

- Divide between two bowls and top with the sliced strawberries and coconut flakes.

- Place in the fridge for 1 hour and then serve garnished with mint leaves.

Peanut Butter and Chocolate Ice Cream Bars

Serves: 15 / Preparation Time: 4 hours and 20 minutes

Nutritional Info per serving:

Calories 227 Net Carbs 5.2 g, Fat 22g, Protein 2.4 g

Ingredients:

1 cup Heavy Whipping Cream

1 tsp Vanilla Extract

¾ tsp Xanthan Gum

⅔ cup Peanut Butter

1 cup Half and Half

1 ½ cups Almond Milk

⅓ tsp Stevia Powder

1 tbsp Vegetable Glycerin

3 tbsp Xylitol

Chocolate:

¾ cup Coconut Oil

¼ cup Cocoa Butter Pieces, chopped

2 ounces Unsweetened Chocolate

3 ½ tsp THM Super Sweet Blend

Directions:

- Blend all of the ice cream ingredients until smooth.

- Place in an ice cream mixture (or not if you don't have one) and follow the instructions.

- Spread the ice cream into a lined pan, and freeze for about 4 hours.

- Combine all of the ingredients in a microwave-safe bowl and microwave until melted. Slice the ice cream bars.

- Dip them into the cooled chocolate mixture.

Raspberry and Coconut Cheesecake

Serves: 12 / Preparation Time: 4 hours and 50 minutes

Nutritional Info per serving:

Calories 263, Net Carbs 5.4 g, Fat 23.1 g, Protein 6.5 g

Ingredients:

2 Egg Whites

¼ cup Erythritol

3 cups desiccated Coconut

1 tsp Coconut Oil

¼ cup melted Butter

Filling:

3 tbsp Lemon Juice

6 ounces Raspberries

2 cups Erythtritol

1 cup Whipped Cream

Zest of 1 Lemon

3 tbsp Lemon Juice

24 ounces Cream Cheese

Directions:

- Apply the coconut oil to the bottom and sides of a springform pan. Line with parchment paper. Preheat your oven to 350 degrees F.

- Mix all of the crust ingredients and pour the crust into the pan.

- Bake for about 25 minutes. Let cool.

- Meanwhile, beat the cream cheese until soft.

- Add the lemon juice, zest, and sweetener.

- In a mixing bowl, beat the heavy cream with an electric mixer.

- Fold the whipped cream into the cheese cream mixture. Fold in the raspberries gently.

- Spoon the filling into the baked and cooled crust. Place in the fridge for 4 hours.

Sugar-Free Chocolate Cake In A Mug

Serves: 2 \ Ready in: 10 minutes

Nutritional Info per serving:

Calories 347, Net Carbs 4.4 g, Fat 29.3 g, Protein 7.2 g

Ingredients:

6 tbsp Coconut flour

¼ tbsp Baking powder

2 tbsp Cocoa powder

1 Egg, beaten

3 tbsp Coconut oil, melted

2 tbsp Stevia

3 tbsp sugar-free Chocolate Chips

A pinch of Salt

Directions:

- Mix coconut flour, baking powder, cocoa powder, stevia, and salt in a microwave-safe mug. Stir in the remaining ingredients until everything is completely moistened. Stir chocolate chips into the batter.

- Microwave for 1 ½ minutes until just firm. Let the cake cool for 2 to 3 minutes before serving.

Vanilla-Chocolate Tofu Pudding

Serves: 2 / Preparation Time: 5 minutes

Nutritional Info per serving:

Calories 577, Net Carbs 8.6 g, Fat 41.1 g, Protein 41.6 g

Ingredients:

1 cup dark chocolate chips

¼ cup Coconut milk

1 tsp Vanilla extract

1 tsp stevia sweetener

1 (14-oz) Firm Tofu

¼ tsp. ground Cinnamon

1 tbsp Coconut flakes

Directions:

- Melt the dark chocolate chips in a microwave-safe bowl for 30 seconds.
- Add the vanilla and ground cinnamon, and transfer to a food processor.
- Add in the rest of the ingredients and mix together until uniform and smooth.
- Pour into cups and refrigerate at least 2 hours.
- Serve sprinkled with coconut flakes.

Chocolate Mocha Ice Bombs

Serves: 6 / Preparation Time: 2 hours and 10 minutes

Nutritional Info per serving:

Calories 232, Net Carbs 5.4 g, Fat 17.3 g, Protein 4.9 g

Ingredients:

½ pound Cream Cheese

4 tbsp powdered Sweetener

2 ounces Strong Coffee

2 tbsp Cocoa Powder, unsweetened

1 ounce Cocoa Butter, melted

2 ½ ounces Dark Chocolate, melted

Directions:

- Combine cream cheese, sweetener, coffee, and cocoa powder, in a food processor.
- Roll 2 tbsp of the mixture and place on a lined tray, you should obtain 6 balls.
- Mix the melted cocoa butter and chocolate, and coat the bombs with it.
- Freeze for 2 hours. Serve chilled.

Saffron and Cardamom Coconut Bars

Serves: 15 / Preparation Time: 3 hours

Nutritional Info per serving:

Calories 143, Net Carbs 2.4 g, Fat 12 g, Protein 2.1 g

Ingredients:

3 ½ ounces Ghee

10 Saffron Threads

1 ⅓ cup Coconut Milk

1 ¾ cups shredded Coconut

4 tbsp Sweetener

1 tsp Cardamom Powder

Directions:

- Combine the shredded coconut with 1 cup coconut milk. In another bowl, mix together the remaining coconut milk with the sweetener and saffron. Let sit for 30 minutes. Heat the ghee in a wok. Add the coconut mixture as well as the saffron mixture, and cook for 5 minutes on low heat, while stirring continuously.

- Stir in the cardamom and cook for another 5 minutes.

- Spread the mixture onto a greased baking pan and freeze for 2 hours. Cut into bars and enjoy!

Almond and Coconut Bark

Serves: 12 / Preparation Time: 1 hour and15 minutes

Nutritional Info per serving:

Calories 161, Net Carbs 2.9 g, Fat 15.3 g, Protein 1.9 g

Ingredients:

½ cup Almonds

½ cup Coconut Butter

10 drops Stevia

¼ tsp Salt

½ cup unsweetened Coconut Flakes

4 ounces Dark Chocolate

Directions:

1. Preheat the oven to 350 degrees F.
2. Place the almonds in a baking sheet and toast for 5 minutes.
3. Melt together the butter and chocolate. Stir in stevia.
4. Line a cookie sheet with waxed paper and spread the chocolate evenly.
5. Scatter the almonds on top and sprinkle with salt.
6. Refrigerate for one hour before serving.

Berry Clafoutis

Serves: 8 / Preparation Time: 45 minutes

Nutritional Info per serving:

Calories 165, Net Carbs 4.9 g, Fat 10.5 g, Protein 5.5 g

Ingredients:

4 Eggs

2 tsp Coconut Oil

2 cups Berries

1 cup Coconut Milk

1 cup Almond Flour

¼ cup Sweetener

½ tsp Vanilla Powder

1 tbsp Powdered Sweetener

Pinch of Salt

Directions:

- Preheat the oven to 350 degrees F.
- Place all of the ingredients, except the coconut oil, berries and powdered sweetener, in a blender. Blend until smooth.
- Grease a flan dish with the coconut oil.
- Pour the mixture into the prepared dish and bake for 35 minutes.
- Sprinkle with powdered sugar and serve.

Homemade Lemon Coconut Ice Cream

Serves: 6 / Preparation Time: 15 minutes + chilling

Nutritional Info per serving:

Calories 256, Net Carbs 5.3 g, Fat 20.1 g, Protein 6.4 g

Ingredients:

4 tbsp Xylitol Sweeteners Barry Farm Foods

Juice and Zest from 1 lemon

3 Eggs

¼ tbsp Tumeric (optional for color)

One 14 oz. can Coconut Milk

Preparation:

- Cool the coconut milk in the fridge overnight. Then, open it and scoop the solid white coconut cream into a bowl. Discard the coconut water.

- Using an electric hand mixer, beat the cream until fluffy and smooth. Add in xylitol, turmeric, lemon juice and zest. Return to the fridge.

- Meanwhile, in two different bowls, separate the eggs whites from egg yolks. Beat the whites until stiff. In the other bowl, whisk egg yolks until light and fluffy.

- Carefully fold egg whites into the yolk mixture.

- Remove the coconut cream from the fridge and lightly stir in the egg mixture.

- Put the bowl in the freezer and give it a stir every 25 - 30 minutes until it reaches the desired consistency. This should take no more than 2 hours.

- With the use of a spatula, rub the inside of the bowl while stirring. If frozen, let sit at room temperature for 10 to 15 minutes before serving.

51578112R00070

Made in the USA
Columbia, SC
19 February 2019